Jack was raised in Brooklyn. When he was 14 years old, one of his uncles took him to Aqueduct Race Track and thus commenced Jack's lifelong love affair with the Sport of Kings. Searching for winners has been Jack's white whale. Jack graduated college in '66. Summers, in college, he worked as a hot walker at Belmont.

After receiving his Master's in Cultural Anthropology, Jack spent the next few years abroad, studying for his Ph.D. at a British University. Two of those four years were spent doing field work in Ste. Luce, a fishing village on Martinique's North East coast.

Eventually, Jack became disenchanted with academia, whereupon he migrated to Wall Street, where he found that his grandmother was correct when she told him, "Rich or poor, it's good to have money." He retired in '98.

Jack lives in a gated community in New Jersey. He spends his time golfing, reading, hanging out at the racetrack, and enjoying time with his family: his lovely wife of 54 years, his three children, their spouses, and what to date are his five grandchildren.

To Everly, Pierce, Cora, Shai, Chloe and any future grandchild who has yet to arrive.

Jack Adler

HORSE RACING: AN OPINION

A New Way of Seeing the Sport of Kings

AUSTIN MACAULEY PUBLISHERS™

LONDON • CAMBRIDGE • NEW YORK • SHARJAH

Ordering Information
Quantity sales: Special discounts are available on quantity purchases by corporations, associations, and others. For details, contact the publisher at the address below.

Publisher's Cataloging-in-Publication data
Adler, Jack
Horse Racing: An Opinion

ISBN 9798886938371 (Paperback)
ISBN 9798886938388 (Hardback)
ISBN 9798886938395 (ePub e-book)

Library of Congress Control Number: 2023921637

www.austinmacauley.com/us

First Published 2024
Austin Macauley Publishers LLC
40 Wall Street, 33rd Floor, Suite 3302
New York, NY 10005
USA

mail-usa@austinmacauley.com
+1 (646) 5125767

Table of Contents

Introduction

The Sapir-Whorf Hypothesis is simple, elegant and utterly profound. It theorizes that language structures reality; that language mediates our perceptions and understanding of reality the same as light entering a prism is defined and refracted into its varying wavelengths. Proof of concept, try and name an entity or emotion for which you have no word. You can't. If one lacks the language to define something, to capture it like a butterfly in one's linguistic net, it does not exist.

Consider the Inuit, Eskimos. They have close to a hundred words to describe snow and ice. They perceive, as they must in order to survive in the harsh, sub-freezing environment in which they dwell, the reality of snow and ice in a far more sophisticated, nuanced manner than an English speaker, whose language offers relatively few words and expressions to grasp the phenomena.

This book is a memoir in which I detail how I see things. Specifically, the concepts and categories that allow me to grasp, understand, and make sense of a particular segment of reality, horse racing. Hopefully, it will allow you, the reader, to see horse racing as I do, through my eyes, so to speak, and in so doing enhance your appreciation of the sport and the relative health of your bankroll.

When I feel especially crafty, sly as a fox, and too clever by half, is when I am most likely to be humbled and brought to my knees. When I attend the races, I try to leave at home as much hubris as possible. If not, I am likely to be raked, as if by machine gun fire, by the slings and arrows of outrageous fortune.

The less ego and emotion involved in one's decision-making, especially at the races, the greater the chances that one will make sound choices, as strong emotions can easily play havoc with the choices one makes, the same as static can weaken and interfere with the clarity of a radio transmission. If you are in a bad mood, angry, irked, bedeviled, or simply bothered and bewildered just a tad or so, it is best to stay home. Trust me, I've learned the hard way.

When it comes to my betting at the racetrack, I have rules, principles if you will, which I try to adhere to. That said, I'm only human, and on occasion I transgress. When I violate one of my taboos, I feel reckless and immature. Same as I would if I stood before a magistrate shamefacedly awaiting my fine for having knowingly made an illegal U-Turn.

Rule number one: there is no such thing as a stone-cold certainty. Like the Tooth Fairy, Santa Claus, and the Easter Bunny, it would be nice if they existed, but they do not. People who believe in 'sure things' are liable to end up wandering in aimless circles, muttering to themselves like outpatients who have gone off their 'meds.' What better example of a sure thing losing than the tortoise and the hare. The hare that day was the ultimate 'lock.' All the tip sheets had the hare as their best bet. Betting the hare was tantamount to betting that the following day the sun would rise in the East. Hare lost. Tortoise won.

Rule Number two: anything can happen. Once, I bet a filly on the grass. She was the only speed and much the best. She was leading by five lengths at the sixteenth pole, going easily and extending her lead with every stride, whereupon, for no discernible reason, she tossed her jockey, leaped over the rail, ran into the infield lake, and drowned. Not only was I stunned by the surreal manner in which I saw a most assuredly winning bet evaporate, but also by the cause of death, drowning, as horses are excellent swimmers. To this day, I am puzzled. It was as if some fundamental law of nature had been suddenly held in abeyance and contravened. It was like watching a bird in mid-flight suddenly forget how to fly and drop from the sky as if made of concrete.

Another example occurred the day the cashier dropped dead. I wanted to make a serious bet on a horse. I couldn't see the horse losing. Two minutes to post time, I handed the cashier my money and called in my bet. The instant before he commenced to punch out my tickets, the cashier's eyes glazed over, and he sagged to the floor. I never got my tickets. The horse won for fun. I was later informed by the authorities that the man had suffered a massive coronary and was dead before he hit the ground. Without proof that I had given their now-deceased employee my hard-earned money, the powers that be refused to return the money I'd wagered, much less the money I would have won. Apparently, my word wasn't good enough. I offered to take a lie detector test. They told me to go away. I said I'd sue. They called security. I left. To the best of my knowledge, it is the only time in my life I've been fucked over by a dead man. Every so often his gaunt, disembodied head haunts my dreams. He's smiling like the cat who swallowed the canary.

If you cannot deal with shit happening, I would strongly advise you not to attempt to win money at the racetrack, as the venue lends itself to strange things happening. If Einstein had hung out at the racetrack, he would never have said, "God does not play dice with the universe." Once you accept the fact that strange stuff happens at the races, oftentimes not to your benefit, it is easier to move forward in a positive mode after you get hammered by fate.

Rule number three: a penny saved is a penny earned. Winning is less about winning than it is about not losing. Not investing in losing tickets is far more important than buying winning ones. I know it sounds like I have things backward, upside down, but I assure you I do not. Most people, to their detriment, try to win by winning more than they lose. I try to win by losing less than I win. Everyone, no matter how astute, is going to suffer losses. The key to coming out ahead is to keep one's losses to a minimum.

Note: Picking a loser is statistically a far more likely occurrence than picking a winner for the simple reason that they are far more abundant. In a 10-horse field, nine horses will lose and only one will win. Therefore, I tread warily when I bet, same as I would if I parachuted into a minefield.

Sometimes I'm in a quandary. To paraphrase Hamlet, "To bet or not to bet, that is the question." When I decide not to bet on a horse and the horse loses, I feel as good, if not better, than if I had won. I breathe a sigh of relief. Same as if I had dodged a bullet. Granted, sometimes the horse I eschewed wins. When this happens, I feel like a bit of a chump. But I get over it real quick because I know that over the long drum roll of my career when all such situations are accounted for, I'll be way ahead.

Rule number four: never bet a horse to do something they have yet to do. When you bet a horse to do something he or she has yet to do, you have moved into the realm of wishing and hoping rather than knowing, which is not a good approach. In order for me to bet a horse to win on the grass, or, let's say, prevail at a mile and a quarter, I must have already seen him do so. I retain the same skepticism toward betting horses to do things they have yet to do as I do toward believing that Yetis, Sasquatches, and the Loch Ness Monster exist. I will not believe they are alive and well and part of our world until one is captured or a dead carcass secured.

Rule number five: the best way to measure a horse's worth, his quality, is in terms of the horses he beats and the style in which he does so. The times he or she runs mean nothing. More about this most important issue later.

Rule number six: don't bet on tips. No matter how good a tip might appear or how real, believable, sincere, and authentic it might seem, it's still just a tip. When I worked as a hot walker, my stable bought a horse, private sale, and shipped him to Belmont, where we were headquartered. The trainer liked him. The owner liked him. His groom was in awe. The horse sizzled in his morning works. We worked him as early as possible in the hope that the clockers would be unaware of his existence, much less the compelling nature of his works. We planned to put him over at a price. The horse was in fine fettle. His coat gleamed as if burnished. He was full of himself, pranced around like he was the second coming. He gobbled up every last oat with alacrity and then looked for more. The jockey said he was a handful and assured us that the horse was sitting on dead ready. Finally, our trainer picked a spot. The night before the race, I was like a child on Xmas Eve. I tossed. I turned. Time crawled. I couldn't wait for the next day to dawn so I could open my present. Only it wasn't wrapped with a big red bow sitting under the family Xmas tree; it was in the fifth at Aqueduct. The morning of the race, the tension in the barn was palpable. We were like a gang of villains about to pull a big heist. The owner and his family were there, all of them dressed to the nines. Clearly, they expected to have their picture taken. The horse went off 23–1. I bet a week's wages. The horse, as expected, ran his eyeballs out. However, he simply wasn't good enough. After a long stretch drive, he lost by half a head. The ride back in the horse van from Aqueduct to Belmont had the same funereal atmosphere as a long, sad ride back from the cemetery after a loved one has been laid to rest. The point is, I had the best of tips. I was in the know, so to speak, from start to finish, and the horse still lost. In other words, if my gardener takes me aside and tells me in hushed, conspiratorial tones that his aunt's close friend overheard at the beauty parlor from her hairdresser that her son-in-law is close friends with a guy who told him that a certain horse can't lose as his first cousin supposedly knows a jockey's agent who owes him a favor, I simply nod my appreciation for the sharing of the confidence and say 'thank you.'

Rule number 7: To understand a race, the best information is acquired by watching it, provided, of course, you know what you are looking at. The line in the Racing Form that represents a race, though valuable to a point, does little justice to what actually transpired. It in no way captures the intangibles: the heart, the grit, the will to win, the class displayed, as they have yet to come up with meaningful metrics to do so.

Rule number 8: Do not bet on a horse that you are not utterly familiar with. I take the same approach to betting on a horse as I do when asked to invest in a business venture. The more due diligence, the more information I have, and the more questions asked and answered to my satisfaction, the better my chances of realizing a positive, profitable outcome. If you think you have a handle on a horse after a race or two, you probably do not.

****

I'm a horse player, a highly specialized seer who attempts through the crystal ball of his opinion to envision a race's outcome and, in so doing, demonstrate as if it were a state of grace, a communion with and understanding of certain elemental truths. It's a ministry of sorts.

A horse race is a collective ritual; a collaboration of horse, horseman, and horse player that both celebrates and expresses certain shared notions of excellence. The rite's cynosure, the thoroughbred, is a collective work of art, a powerful flesh and blood metaphor assiduously sculpted by generations of breeders in tacit agreement as to what constitutes quality. The closer one comes to realizing the ideal, like a Seattle Slew or a Ruffian, the more magic and mythic the symbol becomes.

Horse players hold opinions. The races test their opinion the same as they test a horse's mettle. No two horse players have the exact same opinion. Opinions are unique, like fingerprints. You can learn a lot about a person by parsing their opinion, same as you can by asking them to interpret a blot on a Rorschach test.

Besides the thrill and excitement of winning, the putting of one's ego and money on the line, I go to the racetrack because, in a world that for the most part is predicated on the ongoing production and consumption of plastic, disposable junk, the quality and excellence that a thoroughbred personifies shines like a new penny. There is nothing ticky-tacky about a racehorse. They might not be as smart as dolphins, as cute as kittens, but I find them most edifying.

In '48, the father of a friend of mine inherited, after taxes, four million dollars. It was an awful lot of money at the time. He set aside a sufficient amount to see that his loved ones would always be taken care of and then proceeded to spend the next 42 years at the track. The last time I saw him he was tapped out. Not a penny left. He died soon after. The last thing he ever said to me was, "I'd rather have a lousy day at the track than a good day anywhere else." I'm telling you, horse racing can get in your blood and boil like a fever.

In order for me to win, I have to come out ahead on my serious bets. I take my serious bets seriously. When it comes to serious bets, I am anything but cavalier. I know that if I lose one too many serious bets, I can easily find myself stuck deep in a hole out of which I will have a hard time crawling. Not to say being afflicted with a surfeit of negative emotions, the worst of which is a lack of confidence. All of which can cause me to lose my way and do things I would normally never contemplate, a sure recipe for disaster.

I make other bets, but they're of no consequence. Within the context of my serious bets, they are small potatoes. They have little impact one way or the other on the overall well-being of my bankroll. They simply help ease the passage of time, the same as I do when I twiddle my thumbs.

Either it's a two-dollar bet or a serious bet; there's no in-between.

To attain my end, which is coming out ahead and winning, I spend what some might consider an inordinate amount of time studying horse races in the hope that I will become eminently conversant with the horses involved: their likes, dislikes, proclivities, abilities, affinities, and lack thereof. All too often, though, just when I think I have a handle on a horse, and I can predict with a reasonable degree of certainty how he or she will perform given a certain set of circumstances, they either break down, get shipped out of town, retire to the breeding shed, or lose their form so utterly that whatever I have learned to date is made moot.

I come to my opinion as to a horse's quality and where and when victory might well be in the offing by reviewing their performances according to what I consider to be key criteria, sort of like a drama critic critiquing a play. Every race has any number of compelling storylines that ask the most searching of questions as to the quality and character of its participants. It makes for great theater. At the races, I'm never bored. I'm always engaged, always intrigued.

I make a serious bet when, after performing my due diligence, it becomes apparent that a horse is a 'lock.' When I deem a horse a 'lock,' it means that in all possible scenarios, in my mind at least, his or her winning is a fait accompli, something that will come to pass as if preordained. Trust me, I am fully aware that a horse I consider a 'lock' can lose. All I'm really saying is that when a horse assumes 'lock' status is that I think the probability of his or her winning is so high that I feel in good conscience I can make a serious bet.

When a horse is a 'mortal lock,' it means I like him that much more than if he was just a mere, every day, run-of-the-mill 'lock.' A horse is a 'mortal lock,' it means he has the field at his mercy, the same as a constrictor who has thrown the full measure of his coils around its prey. Still, of course, 'mortal locks' lose the same as regular 'locks.' Just not as often.

In order for a horse to be a 'lock,' mortal or otherwise, it has to pass muster with both my instincts and my intellect. If the two are not in agreement, if there is just a hint of dissonance, no matter how slight, I find it is a good idea to keep my hands in my pockets. When such a situation comes to pass, I'll either watch the race or make a two-dollar bet to help pass the time of day. In other words, vibes count and must be respected, especially bad ones. Picking winners is an art, not a science.

'Locks' don't grow on trees. In terms of their ubiquity, they are more like four leaf clovers. They are few and far between and difficult to discern amid the other blades of grass. If I'm at the track and I start talking with a guy who comes up with a 'lock' every race, I know I am talking to someone who I shouldn't be listening to.

Playing the horses tests a player the same way racing's trials and tribulations test a horse. If you do not do well when adversity accosts you, sometimes in the most hurtful and perplexing of ways, do not go to the race track. Picking winners is not a day at the beach. It's tough. Things can get ugly. You had best be resilient. Also, it is a good idea to realistically manage your expectations. Unrealistic goals can and will engender frustration, which can easily cause one to lose one's poise. This is the most dangerous. When one's poise is in free fall at the race track, one becomes a chicken ripe for the plucking.

The worst thing that can happen is if the first time someone goes to the track, they win. Even worse, they win big. I remember a kid a few years back. Upon collecting after the feature race, he ran around telling everyone how he couldn't believe how easy it was. He referred to the track over and over again as a 'fucking gold mine.' An old timer went over to the kid and asked him if it was the first time he'd been to the races. The kid said it was. The old guy, with a wry, knowing look on his face, shook the kid's hand, gave him an avuncular pat on the shoulder, and said, "Have a good life."

If a 'lock' doesn't stick out as plain as the nose on your face, it's not a 'lock,' not to mention a 'lock' of the 'mortal' variety. A beautiful woman enters a room, you know at first glance if she's beautiful or not. You don't have to think about it. It's the same with a 'lock.' If I find myself wondering if indeed a horse is a 'lock,' it's a sure sign that he or she isn't. I find myself parsing things a tad too much, getting a touch too granular, I back off.

Sometimes it is a good idea not to think too much but to simply rely on your instincts and intuition. When I was a kid and we played ball, when picking sides, we didn't have any stats on which to base our picks. Having seen each other play, we simply knew who was best, second best, and so on and so forth. I'd strongly suggest taking the same approach when deciding which horse you are going to bet on. Trust your instincts. Evolution has honed them for such situations.

When a new kid moved into the neighborhood it took us a few competitions till we knew what he was all about. It was like getting a handle on a 'horse' who had shipped in from out of town.

I'm cautious. I admit it. One of my great fears is ending up a 'stooper.' 'Stoopers' are tapped out. They no longer have any money to bet. Their finances are in such disarray that they can no longer afford to buy the Racing Form. They owe everybody. When they come to the track, they sneak in. Stoopers spend their days at the races, which they watch but don't bet, wandering about, stooping down, picking up and examining tickets that have been discarded. The pot of gold they are looking for is a winning ticket that someone has either inadvertently or mistakenly thrown away. I have yet to see a well-dressed 'stooper.'

Looking for 'locks' is one of my hobbies. Another is golf, and also, I like to read, mostly non-fiction. And fish, which has a lot in common with looking for 'locks.' I'm of the firm belief, a measured confirmation of my life's experiences, that everything can be explained in terms of fishing, fucking, and horse racing; all apt metaphors for any and all aspects of the human condition. I have yet to come across an exception. Think about it.

When I talk about horse racing, I am referring to thoroughbreds, the flats. I'd rather have an anxiety attack than watch, much less bet on, a harness race. The same goes for quarter horses and Arabians. I like watching the jumps, hurdles, but I won't bet on that sort of contest. For me, betting on the jumps is like playing Russian Roulette with a loaded revolver, every fence a potential bullet to the head.

I would also like to emphasize that I'm not a gambler. I'm a horse player. There is a difference. I do not patronize casinos, play cards, speculate in real estate, or bet on sporting events, save, of course, horse races. Also, I'm not wild about the stock market.

Except for the track, the only other venue where I place bets is when I wager on myself when I play golf, same as if I were betting on a horse. It's not just a matter of coincidence that golf enthusiasts refer to a golf course as a track, as in "I played Winged Foot yesterday. It's a really nice track." Horses competing over a racetrack and golfers vying for victory over an 18-hole golf course are the same order of phenomena. The only thing that differentiates the two is the medium over which they engage and the style in which they do so. We understand this loud and clear at an elemental level. Thus the conflation of terminology.

I have yet to come across or hear of anyone who has fed and clothed their family, kept a roof over their heads, paid for their children's college education, and funded their retirement by playing the horses. A long time ago, I knew I wasn't good enough nor had the balls to make my living gambling at the track. Betting on a horse is not all that much fun when paying the rent is contingent on a horse winning a race.

If you are a compulsive sort, tread warily. I've seen bad things happen. People gamble away their homes, lose their family; really ugly stuff.

Because I am acutely aware of my limitations, my goals are modest. At the end of the year, I want the return on my investment to be somewhere around ten percent. If I realize that goal, I am happy as a pig in shit. For those who look down on a paltry ten percent return, all I can say is this, at the end of the year, there are lots of folks out there who would give their nutsack just to be even.

I buy and study the Racing Form five days a week, looking for 'locks' like a prospector panning for gold. Five days a week is enough. It satisfies my needs. Also, I have to give my brain a rest. If I bet every day, bad things happen.

I've been attending the races for over 60 years. Fell in love with the game the first time I went. My uncle took me. At one point, I wanted to be a trainer. In college, during summer vacation, I walked 'hots' at Belmont. Thought it would be my first step toward becoming a trainer. But the Vietnam War was raging, aspiring trainers were not exempted, and so the arc of my life swung off in a different direction. My name, to my everlasting satisfaction, was mentioned in the old Racing Form, the Morning Telegram, known to one and all as the 'Telly,' in Joe Hirsch's column, the man who is without doubt the finest racing scribe of our time. In his column, Hirsch wrote, "Trainer Larry Gieger brags he has the best educated hot walker in the business in reference to recent College grad Jack Adler."

Over the long haul, I'm a loser. It doesn't matter how much I win from here on in; career-wise, I'm a loser. Too much spilled milk, too much water under the bridge. That being said, for the last couple of years, I have been doing okay. Finally!

In order for me to win, I have to grind it out and be very selective as to when and where I make a serious bet. I can't say enough good things about patience. At the racetrack, patience is truly a virtue. When I was younger, I didn't have much. I wanted it all, now. It took a long time before I saw a correlation between the patience I brought to the table and the health of my bankroll. All I can say, better late than never. Now I take great pride in my ability to bide my time while I await my chance, still and patient as an ambush predator. If there is nothing for me to bet on, I don't.

I'm not perfect. I'm only human, and on occasion my patience slips its leash. And when that happens, things can get real ugly, really quick. Just a tad of impatience can wipe out, in the blink of an eye, a month's worth of rectitude. What can I say, on occasion I'm seduced and go chasing after moonbeams.

In order for me to come out ahead, I have to treat the game as a marathon, not a sprint. I have to grind it out. I'm the tortoise, not the hare. There are a lot of good things to be said about immediate gratification, but there is just so much of that to go around. If you try and get more than your fair share, especially at the track, you will get slapped around.

I don't win by making big scores. Why not? I can't. My opinion, my way of seeing things, simply doesn't produce many winners that pay more than five or six to one. It is what it is. And I learned a long time ago that trying to do something that you can't do is not all that productive. Sometimes my horse pays big numbers. But usually that's not the case, and certainly not something to be counted on. I wish my opinion was capable of churning out a steady stream of winners that pay twenty to one or more, but it doesn't. My abilities are what they are, and I have learned to live with them. If I were an athlete, they would say, "He knows his limitations and plays within himself."

Call me picky, overly cautious, lacking flair, if you will, but I can live with those critiques. All I know is that I like the horse racing experience a lot more when I'm cashing tickets, as opposed to when I'm ripping them up. I've been criticized by some of my peers. They say that though my opinion is good, my approach lacks panache, flair, and is overly defensive. What my detractors fail to note or dwell on, which I think is a tad pertinent, is that at year's end, I'm ahead; they're not.

On an average day, I review about 90 races, from which I make two or three serious bets. That's one bet for every 30 or so races carded. Luckily, two or three serious bets a day, along with a couple of two-dollar bets, satisfy whatever craving I might have for action. I feel blessed in this regard.

The entire process takes me, maybe, at most, half an hour.

When I was in Grad School in England I became very friendly with a Postdoc in Mathematics. He was a very proper Englishmen. In fact, I used to go to his house on Sunday afternoons so I could watch him crawling around his garden, gardening, in a white shirt and tie.

He was scary smart. Anyways, one day we were talking and he said something to me that stuck. He said, 'if you know what you're doing it shouldn't take you more than five minutes to solve an equation, no matter how esoteric. "However, if you don't know what you are doing, you can look at the equation till the end of time, and you're still not going to get it right."

With that as context when it comes to solving the problem of solving a race, elucidating its winner, I know what I'm doing. Twenty minutes, at most, reviewing the Racing Form is all the time I need to figure who I intend to wager on that day. If it takes you more time than that, in my opinion you most probably don't know what you are doing.

A race tests one's opinion and one's theories of the racetrack, same as an experiment tests a scientist's hypotheses. The result either confirms or denies the prescience of one's notions. When one's outcomes are more often negative than positive and one finds oneself throwing away more tickets than one is cashing, the race results are telling you in no uncertain terms that your understandings are ill-conceived and are in dire need of rethinking. Losing a race, a negative result, like any failed experiment, provides valuable feedback, the essence of which is that you had better get your shit together. If you don't learn from your mistakes, you are going to keep throwing money away, just as people who don't examine history are supposedly doomed to repeat its mistakes.

A bit of advice: keeping records is of critical importance, obligatory, unless you are a miscreant who thinks ignorance is bliss and prefers to remain uninformed. And unless you are into deluding yourself, honest, accurate records are of greater value than those that are fudged. At a minimum, I record the results and conditions of every serious bet I make. It is valuable data, and one is being foolish if they think they can keep such information in their head. Unless, of course, one is an idiot savant, and I have yet to come across an idiot savant. Not at the racetrack or anywhere else. Apparently, there are just so many idiot savants to go around. I know a lot of strange, bizarre people who hang out at the track, but no idiot savants. I'd like to meet an idiot savant. It's on my bucket list.

Eventually, as one's database grows, patterns inevitably emerge. For example, one learns which races and which conditions are most amenable to one's modes of prognostication. Where one's sweet spots are, and even of greater importance, the sorts of races one should avoid like the plague. If you have an idea as to where the fish are biting and where they are not, you have a better chance of catching your limit.

Not only does my data tell me which races to bet, but it also tells me, as importantly, which betting format is most amenable to providing me with winners. It turns out my world view does not allow me to come out ahead when I bet doubles, make show or place bets, or when I involve myself in the complexities of trying to win via triples, pick fours, pick sixes, parlays, exactas, etc. Therefore, I don't indulge in those sorts of bets, as one definition of insanity is doing the same thing over and over again and expecting a different result.

Turns out the best chance of my winning occurs when I make a plain, old fashioned win bet. Therefore, that's how I roll. If my data told me that three horse exacta boxes were my path to race track nirvana, I'd bet them. But they don't. So I don't. An added plus for me in adopting this approach is that it dovetails quite nicely with my belief that a straight-up win bet is by far the most aesthetically pleasing of all bets. For me, horse playing is about picking winners, the same way for some people, fishing can only mean fly lines and trout.

No disrespect to the Racing Form. It does an excellent job of assiduously collecting and compiling all sorts of valuable information that no one could ever reasonably collect on their own, no matter how diligent. It furnishes the bettor with a lot of good stuff, but in order to know what a horse is all about, there is no substitute for actually watching a horse compete, provided, of course, you know what to look for. If one picture is worth a thousand words, then viewing an entire race from flag fall to finish is worth, minimum, a hundred thousand words, and then some. If your opinion is solely a function of perusing secondary sources like the lines in the Racing Form that reduce a horse's performance to a regimen of symbols and numbers, you are putting yourself at a distinct disadvantage. Nothing beats consulting the primary source, the race itself. Using the form's symbols, numbers, and characters to understand a horse's performance, like any reductionist approach, allows some of the more meaningful aspects of the reality you're studying to escape your purview and slip through your fingers. Same as if you tried to grasp and understand a ballet in terms of a flow chart.

Now for the ultimate rule. Should have mentioned this earlier when I was delineating my rules, but I forgot. I will never, ever bet on a horse unless I consider him or her to be a real, deal race horse, a legitimate, professional sort, a status not easily earned. Just because a horse is competing in a race, do not assume he or she is a professional sort. As a matter of fact, such sorts, relatively speaking, in my opinion, are few and far between. I define a professional sort as a horse who if given a reasonable opportunity to win, will get the job done and prevail. By reasonable opportunity, I mean that if he or she is in form, on a surface they like, at a distance they can handle, against horses they can beat, and the pace is not overly inimical to their interests, they will find their way to the winner's circle. The vast majority of horses do not meet this test. Attaching one's hopes and dreams, not to mention winning money, by wagering on a non-professional sort is beyond foolish.

I try to make a point of watching every race in which a horse I deem a professional sort competes. If someone can come up with a better way of keeping abreast of a horse's form, I'm all ears. In this, the internet era, there is no excuse for not doing so. On average, I end up watching on average maybe six or seven races a day, and maybe ten or eleven on weekends and Holidays. Considering I usually check out between 70 to 100 races a day, it is not all that much. Why? For the simple reason that there are not all that many real-deal, legitimate racehorses out there. Elucidating them is key.

****

The worst loss I've ever suffered occurred when I was a neophyte. Even though the event took place over half a century ago, every last detail is still etched in my mind, as vivid and vibrant as the day it happened. Closure has eluded me. To say I was 'fucked over big time' is a massive understatement.

I loved a horse in the ninth, the back end of a late double. I deemed him to be, a function of my youth and attendant naivete, the 'lock of all locks.' Filled with the high spirits of youth, I tossed caution to the winds and made the most serious bet that I had made to date. It was the equivalent of my monthly salary at the time. I wheeled all the horses in the eighth with my 'mortal lock' in the ninth. Those days I bet daily doubles. The feature, the eighth, was won by the longest shot in the race. The horse went off 43 –1. I was now alive in the ninth with a horse I deemed unbeatable. If my horse won the ninth, I would win what, at the time, would have been close to half a year's salary. All tax-free, I might add.

My 'lock' in the ninth had all the speed and went right to the front. As there was no other early foot in the race, he had it all his own way and paid no price for the lead. Much to his benefit, he set a slow, leisurely pace. Glacial fractions that took nothing out of him. Despite the languid pace, he kept putting more and more daylight between himself and his pursuers, all of whom were running like a herd of cripples. I loved it. At the half-mile pole, my horse was six lengths clear, going easy on his own, his jockey sitting still as a statue. As they straightened for home, he commenced to accelerate ever so slightly, again all on his own, without being urged. With every jump, his lead widened. The horses behind him appeared stapled to the racing surface. At the eighth pole, he was 15 lengths clear of the field, pulling away, extending his lead with each and every stride. At the sixteenth pole, he was 20 lengths to the good. I commenced to decide where exactly I would vacation in the Caribbean. It came down to either Martinique or St. Lucia, neither of which I knew anything about. I was simply entranced by the exoticism of their names. Also, they made me think of pirates and swashbucklers, and after this score, I most assuredly would be considered a kindred spirit.

The last jump before the wire, my horse snapped a leg and went down in a heap. His jockey sailed over the colt's neck and actually crossed the finish line. The rules, however, clearly state that in order to be declared the winner, the jockey has to have the horse under him, in his possession, so to speak, when breaking the plane of the finish line. The horse I'd bet on writhed about in abject agony as he tried in vain to regain his footing. It wasn't a pretty scene. The others swerved around him like vehicles trying to avoid a traffic accident. They put the horse down, then and there, a foot or two from the finish line.

I think I was the last person to leave the track that day. I just stood there and stared in disbelief, gobsmacked to the nth degree. Upon arriving home, numb with disbelief, I took to my bed and, for the next several days, laid there with the covers pulled tightly over my head, save for when I went to the bathroom to answer nature's call. I didn't eat. I couldn't. I had no appetite. I didn't make a bet for almost two weeks.

∗∗∗∗∗∗∗∗∗∗∗∗∗∗∗∗∗∗∗∗∗∗∗∗∗∗

All of which makes me think of luck, good and bad, both of which abound at the racetrack. I've had good luck. I've had bad luck. It's good to be good, but it is far better to be both lucky and good. I define luck as the catchment into which flows all that is inexplicable, random, devoid of rhyme or reason, defies rational explanation, and where neither cause nor correlation can be discerned. When we move past the borders of our understanding, we call it luck.

Apparently, the same randomness and uncertainty that characterize the quantum world of subatomic particles often finds expression at the racetrack.

If only I could get a handle on luck, figure it out, I'd be stretched out on a chaise lounge, sunning myself on my fully staffed yacht off the coast of Monaco, a cigar in one hand, an ice-cold bottle of beer in the other, surrounded by a bevy of young lovelies clad in skimpy, revealing bikinis, all vying for my favors.

Some explain luck as the residue of design. Notice that they only come to this conclusion after whatever it is that they are explaining has transpired. In other words, the notion is unabashed hindsight. Until someone can point out to me beforehand that something will happen before it does, like a particular horse will win a race, because of the residue of some design they've apprehended, I'll take 'luck is the residue of design' with a grain of salt, same as I do other platitudes like 'nice guys finish last,' or 'the meek shall inherit the earth.'

Anyone plays a hunch; they need their head examined. Hunches taunt luck; spit in luck's eye; and if you spit in luck's eye, it will spit right back, only a lot harder. It's like baiting a bear.

Anyone who doubts the existence of luck, both good and bad, and its whimsical and capricious nature, please explain the following. Two guys are walking along, chatting, when all of a sudden, out of the blue, a meteorite hits one in the head, kills him, and the other fellow walks away unscathed. If you can come up with a reasonable, plausible explanation as to why one of the two gentlemen was sent to the 'great beyond' and the other walked away without a scratch, please let me know. I'd be more than interested. Luck is always out there, always in play, lurking. It's naive to think otherwise.

Though I don't really buy into the whole religion thing, every so often, in order to attract good luck and keep bad luck at bay, I find myself praying. It's like hedging a bet.

Some people try and get lucky by finding four-leaf clovers. Others don't let black cats cross their path. Still others investigate the planets and how they are aligned. For reasons for which I do not have a clue, I have certain hard and fast rituals that I believe, if I adhere to them, will keep bad luck from ringing my doorbell. To wit, I don't park in handicapped spaces, make fun of the dead unless they were complete assholes, I don't tell my dreams before breakfast, and I will not own a green car. Once, on vacation, I leased, sight unseen, a car. It turned out to be green. I tried to exchange it. All they had were green cars. For one dreadful week, I had to drive a green car. I felt like I had a target on my back. I kept waiting for the other shoe to fall. Luckily, nothing untoward happened. I haven't been in a green car since. It's my belief that I have no green car luck left. Used it all up that week.

I do have a lucky number, seven. I was born on July 7, the seventh day of the seventh month. I shared my birthday with my father. He, too, was born on the seventh day of the seventh month. Also, Mickey Mantle's number was seven.

But at the races, lucky numbers mean nothing. The only number that really matters is the amount of dollars you have in your pocket at any given moment.

I figure that luck comes into play at the racetrack and has an impact on one's winning or losing maybe one in twenty races. As to how I arrived at that number, all I can say is that I have been playing the horses for over 60 years, and one out of twenty seems right to me. Luck is not a science.

One in twenty, five percent, perhaps not all that much, but still, I'd rather have the five percent on my side. I certainly don't want it working against me. Like good old home cooking, there is nothing quite as tasty as plain old dumb luck. Toward achieving that end, enjoying good luck at the racetrack. I have a whole special set of behaviors I use at the track in the hope that it will entice good fortune to shine its light on me and keep bad luck at bay. I keep my money tucked in my right pants pocket, my bankroll folded over in half, with the edges of the bills all in neat, perfect alignment. One dollar bills on top, followed respectively by fives, tens, twenties, fifties, and hundreds. If my money is not configured in that manner, not only do I feel unlucky but extremely uncomfortable as well, and I rectify the situation as soon as I can, the same as I would if my underwear got stuck up my butt crack.

Also, at the racetrack, I never carry any spare change on my person, as I believe doing so brings bad luck. As to how and why I have come to this conclusion, I have no idea. If I receive change when I cash a ticket or from a vendor when I get a beer, a chocolate bar, a cigar, or whatever, I throw the change away, discreetly, of course. Don't want anyone to think I'm not playing with a full deck. At the track, only money in my pocket is made out of paper. When I'm not at the races, I don't care how many pennies, dimes, nickels, etc. I might have on my person. At the racetrack, though, change is taboo. Once I got nosed out. Serious bet. My horse was much the best but he clipped heels turning for home, gallantly righted himself, and commenced a renewed drive up the rail. Twice the rail opened, then just as quickly shut, thwarting him both times. With no other options left, he then wheeled to the outside, gathered himself yet again, quickened considerably, only to lose by bob of the head. A horrible outcome for a horse that was much the best. I put my hands in my pocket. Felt a dime. Need I say more?

If you ask me the origins of these beliefs, I'll shrug. I have no explanation, none. I just do it because it feels right. Also, I think it works. Like luck, it's not rational. The only way, I believe, to deal with that which is random and irrational is to deal with it irrationally. Behaving rationally is simply not going to get the job done.

A myth about luck that some propagate is that luck, good or bad, evens out. Not so. It should, being the apotheosis of that which is random, but it doesn't. One time I made a serious bet on a horse that was 14–1. Such opportunities are few and far between. The horse wins but gets disqualified and placed second for what I and others perceive to be a whisper of a foul. I'm pissed. My friend, Mook, tells me, "No big deal, just bad luck. Don't worry. In the end, it all evens itself out." Okay. Two weeks later, I have a $2 bet on a filly that is 4–5. A bet I make just so I can watch the race. I think she's the best and that she's going to win, but not to the extent that I think she's worth a serious bet. And it would be stupid to bet against her, as I really can't see any of the others taking her measure. Clearly, it is a twiddling my thumbs type of bet. I bet two dollars. She loses and comes second. The winner was disqualified and placed second for an egregious foul that almost knocked the filly off her feet at the 1/16th pole. The filly is put up. I won one dollar and 40 cents. I happen to be with Mook, the same fellow I was with when I got taken down two weeks ago when I made a serious bet that went off 14–1 and lost. He tells me, "See, it evens out, just like I told you." I look him in the eye. Is he kidding? No. He's dead serious. I walk away so as to assure myself that I do not say something I'll regret.

Bennie is Mook's best friend. You rarely see one without the other. They were the best man at each other's weddings. Bennie is bright. He has a Master's Degree in Political Economy. His Master's thesis, "How the Boer War Impacted Sardine Prices in Estonia". Bennie knows more about sardines, Estonia, and The Boer War than anyone I know. Bennie wanted to go into politics. Be a consultant. Manage elections for right-minded individuals like himself. He ended up buying and running a brick oven pizza place.

Mook's real name is Richie. Once I called him by his real name, Richie. He didn't respond. I was puzzled. Bennie immediately set me straight. "He's the Mook. He doesn't respond to Richie". That clarified, he told me that the reason he is called Mook is because he looks like a fucking Mook.

This bit of information didn't help me in the least because I have no idea what a Mook should look like. Mook is the only Mook I've ever met. Apparently, Mooks, like Idiot Savants, are few and far between.

To me, The Mook is an average-looking guy, a cigar always in his mouth who looks out at the world through a pair of glasses with extra-thick lenses.

Talk about being in the wrong place at the wrong time. Once we were sitting in the back having a few beers. Bennie asked me to switch seats so he could have a better view of the toteboard. Thirty seconds after we changed seats Bennie got walloped in the face by a substantial amount of bird shit. If he hadn't asked me to switch seats, it would have been me who got shit on. A classic case of 'for the grace of God go I'.

One guy I know says it's good luck to get laid the night before he goes to the track. His wife dreads my phone calls; as the only time I ever call is to ask him if he wants to go to the races. Another of my acquaintances, to avoid bad luck, has a double shot of Johnny Walker Black, neat, before he goes to the windows for his first bet of the day. I know another guy, a real oddball, who never watches a race live. Race begins, he shuts his eyes, hides behind a pillar, his back to the track, and listens to the call. Afterward, he has no problem watching the replay over and over again. But he won't watch the race live. "Nothing good," he says, "can come of it."

I use the word key a lot. Keys are important. A key gets to the nub of things. A horse player is only as good as the keys he comes up with. Coming up with the right key(s) is, well, key.

When I do a postmortem after a loss, which is always, I look for the key or perhaps keys to explain why a horse performed as he did, sort of like a medical examiner searching for a cause of death. Losing bets are more likely to provide a teachable moment than winning ones. If nothing went awry and things unfolded as you thought they would, then there is nothing to investigate. It's only when things do not go according to plan that something of pertinence might be revealed and another piece of the puzzle revealed.

The path to financial ruin is paved with bad keys. If you conclude that a horse lost a race because of the distance, when in fact it was the pace that was the key to his failure, the next time the horse runs at that distance, you will have placed yourself at a disadvantage. Not only won't you bet on the horse in question, but you might well bet against him and lose.

Knowing the key before the race, not afterward, is what separates the men from the boys.

People differ in terms of their cognitive abilities. Meaning some people are smarter than others. The smarter someone is, the more likely it is that they will find the correct solution to a race and come up with the winner than someone who is somewhat dimmer. I'm of the opinion that I do okay at the race track because there are a lot of people out there who are dumber than me. Obviously, there are people out there who are far smarter and more sophisticated than yours truly. To them, I'm the dumb money. Someone to be taken advantage of. That's okay; I'll take my chances.

Class

A thoroughbred's career is a series of tests formatted as races, the results of which define him; it's the clay from which his legacy is molded. Of all the qualities for which a horse is tested, none is more important than class.

Class is the heart and soul of racing. A ramifying theme, it resonates throughout. All things being equal, by definition, the class of the field always wins. Class, like cream, always rises to the top.

'Class will out' is an oft-used expression bandied about at the racetrack. For most horseplayers, the notion is unimpeachable, the same as a religious precept. It means that when a horse has class, he is holding all the trump cards. A horse can have 'winning ways,' run like the wind, have the stamina of a champion, but if he or she lacks class, those other attributes will remain moot.

More than any other factor, a horse's class determines the level at which he or she will be able to successfully compete. If a professional, legitimate sort has the class of a cheap claimer, that's the level where he or she will be able to succeed, no matter what other traits they might have been endowed with.

Of all a horse's attributes, a horse's class is the one that I wish to be most conversant with.

Class is a trait that can be passed from one generation to the next. You can't teach or train a horse to have class; either he has it or doesn't. Of all the traits a thoroughbred is bred to express, none is more prized and revered than class.

When breeders say they 'breed the best to the best and hope for the best,' what they are really saying is that they 'breed the classiest to the classiest and hope for the classiest.'

Take note: the fastest horse is not necessarily the classiest. He might be. But then again, he might not. Class and speed are separate, distinct qualities. Given a choice between having a horse with a surfeit of class or athletic ability, one or the other, I'll opt for the former. It's a non-issue, a no-brainer. Speed without class is of no pertinence. It's a horse's class that gives his athletic ability its backbone and with it that which enables him or her to win. Without the grit a horse's class provides, whatever God-given ability to run a horse has been gifted with will be rendered moot. I've seen horses who could run like the wind but couldn't win a race if their lives depended on it. Why? Little to no class.

Of all the concepts spoken of and referred to at the racetrack, none is used as often or is as poorly understood as class. Class, simply put, is the relative ability of one horse to dominate and impose his will upon the other. One way a horse displays his dominance, that he's the boss, in charge, the alpha, is by being in front and controlling the pace. Leaders lead. Followers follow. By being in front, leading, a thoroughbred asserts his dominance.

When a horse is on the lead at the wire, we say he won. If we could converse with a thoroughbred, he would most probably say, "I dominated."

When one horse allows another to lead and himself to be led, it is an act of submission; an acknowledgment and acceptance of his subordinate status, the same as a serf bowing to the Lord of the Manor.

People have lots of ways of describing class, thus some of the confusion. When a horse is said to be determined, game, having heart, character, mettle, showing resolve, holding on like a bulldog, neither willing to give way or be denied, it is his class, his ability to dominate and bend others to his will that is being referred to.

At the other end of the spectrum, when a horse is referred to as having the heart of a pea, being a rat, gutless, a quitting dog, possessing the balls of a mosquito, etc., it is his lack of class, his inability to dominate, hold sway, and impose his will that is being flayed with pejoratives.

The less class a horse has, the greater his inability to stamp his will upon another.

When I was a little boy, my friends and I often played a game called King of the Hill. A simple game, we played it on a slight, grassy uplift of ground on one of the vacant lots that dotted the neighborhood. The goal of the game, gain control of the hill's topmost part, claim it, so to speak, and then repulse any and all challengers that sought to push you off the high ground and usurp and assume your position of preeminence.

It was great fun. Especially after it had rained. I mean, what could be more fun for a nine-year-old than an afternoon spent rollicking about in the mud, slipping and sliding, pushing and shoving and wrestling as we tested one another to see who would eventually take control and emerge as the King of the Hill.

I see the childhood game of King of the Hill as an apt metaphor not only for horse racing but for any and all of the games and competitions in which humanity engages. When one of us stood alone atop the hill, it was the same as a horse being in front, leading. In my opinion, I see no substantive difference between little boys pushing and shoving each other in order to gain command of the Hill, and thoroughbreds tussling and battling for control of the lead. A game of King of the Hill concluded when one of us was finally able to achieve through his strength and determination unchallenged dominion over the hill by discouraging and demoralizing the others until all thoughts of their trying to supplant and topple the current 'King' had vanished. When someone stood atop the hill, alone and unchallenged, it was the same as a horse being in control of the lead at the wire. In both, the winner had bossed the others, taken command, and bent them to his will.

Thoroughbreds maintain, as do all social animals, a hierarchical system of relationships based on the relative ability of one animal to dominate the other, with the 'top dog,' so to speak, at the apex. In common parlance, such a system of relationships is referred to as a 'pecking order.' Among thoroughbreds, for which dominance has been assiduously bred, the need to dominate and battle over rank has been magnified and attenuated to the point that it is one of the focal points of their social life.

From an evolutionary point of view, a pecking order is a positive adaptation in that it supplies the group with a built-in chain of command that allows its members to respond to external threats in quick, efficient fashion as the subordinate animals spurred by their instincts will defer to the more dominant animal and follow his or her lead.

The pecking order also provides a mechanism whereby breeding privileges are delineated in such a manner that the most dominant animals end up breeding with the greatest frequency. This ensures that the gene pool from which subsequent generations will be fashioned is composed of the genetic material of those strong, fit, intelligent, assertive, robust sorts best suited to survive evolution's trials and tribulations.

Horses, sheep, cattle, wolves, zebras, lobsters, walruses, elephants, goats, chimps, dolphins, homo sapiens, alligators, chickens, and the list goes on and on, all maintain 'pecking orders to one degree or another.'

As a social model, the ubiquity of pecking orders existing among such varied and diverse species attests to the advantages it confers. If it did not, species that constantly were structuring themselves into such hierarchies would be culled and consigned to history's dustbin, the same as a thoroughbred with knock-knees.

All species that maintain pecking orders employ a repertoire of highly ritualized behaviors, patterned as stylized combats, that enable the group's individuals to sort themselves out and establish their relative rank. Rams butt heads, hens literally peck at one another, stag locks horns, pigs bite each other's backs, fighting cocks fight, swordsmen duel, and thoroughbreds race.

Race horses do not race to see who is fastest; they race to see who is best, with best being defined as the classiest, the most dominant, the race being the mechanism, the process, whereby that question is answered. Being able to run fast certainly aids one in establishing hegemony over others. However, no matter how fast a horse can run, if he lacks the requisite class, he will lack the wherewithal to dominate, and be in front, in command, leading at the wire.

All things being equal, a less dominant horse, no matter how fast, will always finish in arrears of a less athletic but more dominant, classier foe.

When people engage in rituals to establish hierarchies, pecking orders, we say that they are 'playing games.' The urge and need to play games, to rank ourselves in any and all social contexts is hard-wired into us, same as our gift of language and our opposable thumbs. Expecting homo sapiens not to constantly construct relationships based on hierarchies, no matter the social context, would be like expecting birds not to fly.

The impulse to rank and dominate is expressed at all levels of our social integration. From putting someone down at a cocktail party with an especially trenchant remark to nations going to war.

When games are played within a formal, structured environment governed by a codified set of rules, we call it sport. Teams, like an individual, can be dominated. Dominated teams are said to be demoralized, to have lost heart.

All our institutions mirror various aspects of who and what we are, the human condition. Horse racing speaks to us about games and the manner in which we fashion the myriad, necessary hierarchies that permeate our social lives.

Not surprisingly, as horse racing images and metaphors so aptly capture the phenomena of such competitions, the ubiquity of the language used to connote it is freely used, migrating as it were, to describe the playing of games in any and all contexts. A highly competitive event is referred to as a 'real horse race,' be it as diverse a competition as a Presidential election or a keenly contested spelling bee. Vying competitors, no matter the competition, "get out of the gate quickly, make a run, win by a nose, chomp at the bit, spit the bit, show no heart, get caught at the wire," etc.

In addition, people are said to 'jockey for position.' Where? Within all the myriad hierarchies that structure our social life.

Though correlation does not necessarily prove causation, when correlations abound, it can well suggest that something is indeed afoot. With this as context, it's my belief that thoroughbred racing evolved from the medieval sport of jousting. Both are highly ritualized combats. Both involve mounted riders. Knights carry their Liege Lord's colors into battle, same as a jockey sports his owners' silks. Trumpets sound the call to battle. Given the similarity in terms of its varied elements, style, manner, pageantry, pomp, and the other grace notes of chivalry they both express, it is my belief that horse racing evolved from and supplanted jousting when the spectacle of men battering themselves senseless, often with fatal consequences, became unacceptable to the sensibilities of the elite. Bottom line: thoroughbreds became our Knights in shining armor.

As far as games go, I see little meaningful difference between Knights jousting and little boys playing King of the Hill. Knights demonstrate their prowess by unseating their rivals, little boys dominate their rivals by pushing them off the hilltop.

And I imagine that at these long-ago festivals where jousting Knights were the feature attraction, many in attendance harbored strong opinions as to which Knight was best. It certainly does not lack credulity to imagine one spectator offering his opinion to another as to who he liked in an upcoming joust. I can easily see one fellow sidling up to another and saying to another, "See the guy over there with the red eagle on his shield. I saw him practice the other morning. He was awesome. I can't see him losing. I think he's a lock in the next tilt."

There is little difference between a pit bull, a fighting cock, and a racehorse. The differences are in style, their aesthetic. In their battle to dominate, pit bulls and fighting cocks draw blood. Thoroughbreds dominate in a more genteel fashion; they race. Bottom line: a thoroughbred is a rich man's fighting cock.

Once, leafing through a magazine, I came across a picture of Triple Crown winner Affirmed and his groom. Just below, a different story, there was a picture of a champion pit bull straining against his leash. Both Affirmed and the pit bull appeared to be cut from the same bolt of cloth; Affirmed a dark chestnut, the pit bull a deep, rich mahogany. The pair looked out at the world with unflinching, imperious eyes, same as Noblemen surveying their domain. Both sets of ears were cocked as if on high alert, as if awaiting some as yet unseen challenge. Their coats shone as if burnished. Both exuded overweening pride, confidence, and poise. Both thoroughbred and pit bulls had their feet firmly planted and their chests thrust defiantly outward. And both gave the distinct impression that nothing would have made them happier than to be released and ushered into some fray so they might do battle and be the warrior they were bred to be and of course, it goes without saying, demonstrate who was in charge.

When a thoroughbred is in front, leading, he is proclaiming that he is in charge, the alpha, the boss. It's like a gorilla pounding his chest, a cock crowing, or a snorting bull pawing the earth. If another horse takes issue with the assertion that the horse on the lead is making, which is that he's best, in charge, the boss, it is incumbent upon him to challenge and wrest the lead, and in so doing demonstrate that he is preeminent, the leader, the boss, that he is not one to follow, and that the other, not he, will be the one to bend the knee.

A thoroughbred challenges and displaces the leader; he then becomes the hunted. In order for him to maintain his newly acquired status, he must now turn back all subsequent challenges. And so it goes. The King's head, when it is on the lead, never rests easy.

A key difference between racehorses and little boys playing King of the Hill resides in the fact that if a lad is beaten back in his attempt to take the hill, he might well regroup and make several subsequent attempts. Not so with thoroughbreds. Once a racehorse is 'hooked' by another and 'put away,' shown their place in the scheme of things, he or she will rarely challenge again. Nine times out of ten, once a horse is put away, he stays 'put away' and ceases to be a factor. If and when a horse who has been seemingly 'put away' launches yet another challenge, he is said to 'have come again.' When a horse 'comes again' take note, as only horses with more than a touch of class will do so.

When a horse quickens, looms alongside another, looks him in the eye, and challenges for the lead, it is a provocation, an act of aggression, the same as the throwing down of a gauntlet, knocking the chip off someone's shoulder, or asking someone to step outside.

It is then and there, when horses 'hook up,' and look one another in the eye, that we find out where the muffins are hidden. Much of racing's dramatic tension, that which rouses its aficionados to their feet, clamoring for more, occurs at that moment of truth when horses throw down, look one another in the eye, and in so doing plumb and reveal their respective quality and worth.

When horses 'hook up,' dig in, and race side by side, head to head, eye to eye, they are taking one another's measure, communicating to one another their relative strength, ability, and most of all, their will. It is the same sort of communication that takes place with prize fighters. Only prizefighters speak with their fists; every punch given and received an unspoken yet clearly understood message.

Eventually, after 'hooking up,' battling, ding donging it eye to eye, one of the combatants will stamp his will upon the other, and a tacit understanding is reached as to who is in charge and thus who will lead. Once a horse is 'outclassed,' made to understand his station in the pecking order, he acknowledges his subordinate role and his limitations by ceasing to challenge. The fight taken out of him, he shows his acquiescence by retiring from the fray and allowing himself to be led. It is an act of fealty, an acknowledgment that he knows his place, the same as a vanquished warrior ceding his sword to his conqueror. The horse backing off, the one that has been 'put away' does so because he intuitively understands that he is out of his depth and will not be able, no matter how hard he might try, to take the measure of the horse he has 'hooked.'

Class is a relative concept. The only way to calibrate a horse's class is to decipher what transpires when horses 'hook up,' as it is then and there that their relative class, their place in the 'pecking order is illuminated'. As per rule number five, the only way to measure a horse's quality is in terms of the horse he bests and the style in which he does so.

How grimly and grudgingly do the combatants do battle? How long do they stay 'hooked' before one of them gives way, concedes, and retires? Take careful note of the manner in which the concession is offered: is it a slow, grudging, grim inch-by-inch erosion of will, or is it a sudden spitting of the bit and going backward as if shot? The more dramatic the concession and the quicker it is made, the greater the disparity in class between the two combatants.

Also, I would respectfully direct you to pay attention to a jockey's mode of behavior when one mount 'hooks' another. How hard does he have to work to put it the other way? Is it done with mild urging, a hand ride, or does he have to scrub his horse hard and take to the whip?

It is also critical that when horses 'hook up,' the ensuing battle's dynamic be perceived and understood within the context of the pace that preceded it, something I will go into in greater detail in a subsequent chapter.

As a general rule of thumb, all things being equal, the easier one horse puts way another, the classier he is. The more evenly matched the protagonists, the longer they will stay 'hooked.' Racing's finest moments occur when evenly matched horses of great quality, horses who are loath to give an inch 'hook up' and engage. See Affirmed and Alydar, Gun Bow and Kelso, Sunday Silence and Easy Goer, etc. Check them out on YouTube. You will be enthralled.

Any confrontation where race horses 'hook up' offers valuable understanding as to their relative quality. I pay as much attention to parsing what transpires when horses are 'hooked up' battling for place or show as I do for those vying for the lead. I've seen many intense, gallant battles fought long after the winner has crossed the finish line as two trailers battle to see who will out game and lead the other. It's what race horses do.

Jockey Donald Pierce put it best when asked if his Derby mount that year, Flying Paster, was as good as Affirmed, the previous year's winner. Pierce laconically replied, "I don't know; he's never hooked Affirmed."

To put a human face on the phenomenon of what transpires when horses 'hook up,' I pose the following question: How long would you have to be 'hooked up,' exchanging punches with Mike Tyson, before you realized your chances of winning were nil? Two, maybe three seconds. When a boxer is 'put away,' he throws in the towel.

Put away, put down, put in one's place, it's all the same. These are the dynamics by which hierarchies are built.

How many Sandy Koufax fastballs would you flail at before you knew he was in command and that you had no chance of putting the bat on the ball, much less getting a hit? Or if you 'hooked' Bill Buckley in a debate, how much back and forth would have to take place before you realized your point of view was not going to prevail? How many of Roger Federer's ground strokes would you have to receive before it dawned on you that you weren't going to win a point, much less a game, a set, or a match? Or if you 'hooked' Gary Kasparov in a game of chess, how many moves would have to be made before you realized you were competing against a far, far better class of chess player and your chances of winning were nonexistent? Chess players moving pieces are the same order of phenomena as fighters exchanging punches or 'hooked up' race horses looking one another in the eye as they take one another's measure.

Years back, I played a game of chess against the world champion and 'hooked' him, so to speak. He was giving an exhibition. He played sixty people simultaneously, of whom I was one. Not that I earned a seat at the table because I was that good a chess player, but rather because it was a charity affair and I showed up with the requisite cash to buy a seat at the table. The Champion's only condition was that he played white and the opposition black. He simply walked from one board to the other, took note of the position, made his move, and then moved on to his next opponent. He was most impressive. He lost one game, tied two, and won 57. It was, to say the least, a dominating performance. My defeat was swift and merciless. After maybe ten or twelve moves, my position was hopelessly constricted, and it was eminently apparent I had no good moves. I had no chance. I knew it. He knew it. And he knew that I knew that he knew. Rather than continue on, tilting fecklessly at windmills for no good reason, I resigned, and toppled my King with a flick of my forefinger.

My experience with the world's premier chess player and my intuitive understanding that I had no chance whatsoever after exchanging a few moves with him is not that much different than what happens when a cheap claiming horse 'hooks up' with a horse that has the class of a champion. A mediocre horse 'hooks up' with, let's say, Seattle Slew, it does not take him all that long before he understands with crystal clarity who's in charge, whereupon he concedes the issue, backs off and is 'put away.' Noted trainer Preston Burch aptly describes the reality when he says, "A horse has class, or he does not…a horse who has it needs to run a mere few hundred feet head-to-head with a horse who does not, and the latter will pull himself up like a man slamming down the brakes on an automobile." It's what people are referring to when they say, "class will out."

A cheap horse 'hooks' a far classier foe and quickly ceases to compete; it is as if the classier, more dominant horse has thrown some psychic switch that short circuits the other's resolve.

When horses 'hook up,' they look one another in the eye. It is aggressive, belligerent behavior. Its intent is to intimidate and demoralize, and convey to the other that they are not to be trifled with.

When I worked as a hot walker, I had the good fortune of getting to know John Nerud, the maestro who trained Dr. Fager. In my opinion, Dr. Fager was the best racehorse I ever laid eyes on. And it is not even close. But more about that later. As I type these words, looking down on me from my bulletin board is a wrinkled, cracked, black-and-white photograph of John Nerud and Dr. Fager. Written in the lower left-hand corner, it says, 'To Jack, one of my biggest fans, best of luck, your buddy, Dr. Fager.' It was given to me by Mr. Nerud over 60 years ago, and I value it greatly. In the picture, Mr. Nerud, as I always addressed him, is standing to Dr. Fager's left, holding his shank.

Mr. Nerud once told me that by the time Dr. Fager made it from the walking ring onto the racetrack, his eyes, pumped up by his competitive juices and his need to dominate and impose his will, seemed to literally double in size as he prepared to do battle. He described Dr. Fager's eyes as 'being ablaze' as 'the good Doctor,' as he referred to him, readied himself to put the fear of God into any horse that had the temerity to look him in the eye. Mr. Nerud said, "Any horse that looked Dr. Fager in the eye was sure to die." However, it rarely happened that another horse got to look at Dr. Fager in the eye. Why? Because besides being class personified, Dr. Fager was also the fastest, most athletic horse I have ever seen, and it is tough to look a racehorse in the eye that you can't catch up to.

To grasp the impact that looking an opponent in the eye can have on one's ability to compete, imagine you're scheduled to fight Sonny Liston. I guarantee that for all practical purposes at the weigh-in when standing chest to chest with Liston, eye to eye with his baleful, menacing visage, whatever resolve you might have had would melt away as your instincts told you that doing battle with Mr. Liston was not a brilliant idea. The same way a horse would feel if he looked Dr. Fager in the eye.

There is a reason why, when riding the subway late at night, it is a good idea to make only the most fleeting sort of eye contact with your fellow passengers. Forging long-term eye contact, or staring, can lead to bad things happening, as it is a primordial mode of aggression and may well be answered in kind.

A horse race is over when all the entrants, save one, the horse controlling the lead, have been put away. Once a horse has established his dominion and inculcated among the others the notion that challenging him is futile, the race for all intents and purposes is over, and that horse can, if he so wishes, set as slow a pace as he desires, as no matter how slow he goes, none of the others, even if they are capable of running faster, will attempt to garner the lead as they know that mounting a challenge is pointless, as they know in their heart of hearts, that it be will be rebuffed.

I've seen many a race where a horse established dominance early, bossed the others, and took complete and total command within the first quarter mile, whereupon the rest of the race became as competitive as a parade.

No one is ever going to make the case that a thoroughbred is the brightest light in the animal kingdom. But when it comes to matters of dominance, who is, who isn't, and to what degree, they possess a unique, uncanny ability. It's bred into them, as deep and intractable as a nail hammered into a two-by-four.

I'm a big believer that the true measure of a person is how he or she deals with adversity. Same for racehorses. The more class a horse has, the more punishment and adversity he can absorb and overcome. A horse limited in his ability to deal with adversity is vulnerable, same as a prizefighter with a glass jaw. The less dominant a horse, the easier he can be discouraged and succumb when adversity rears its head. Cheap horses are like people who call in sick when they have the sniffles.

For a thoroughbred, adversity can take many forms: too much weight, repeated challenges that require repelling, getting left at the gate, being blocked, forced wide, being the victim of a disadvantageous pace, a poor ride, etc. For Alydar, it was Affirmed.

Any horse can look like a champion when everything goes his or her way. It's only when adversity rears its head that we find out what a horse is really made of. Just how classy he or she is.

To understand what I am referring to, go to YouTube and watch Forego, compete in the '76 Marlboro Cup. For Forego, three-time horse of the year, the race was littered with adversity. It had rained the night before and drizzled that morning. The track was off, somewhere between sloppy and good. I was surprised the big gelding didn't scratch, as he did not do his best running when the track was off. 'The Mighty One' is my racetrack cronies and I referred to him showed best when the footing was firm and fast.

We referred to him as the 'Mighty One' not just because of his fiery, indomitable will but also because of his size. He was about as big and sturdy as a racehorse gets. Up close, in the walking ring, he would tower over the others, and it appeared as if he were the product of someone taking two horses and scotch-taping them together. Forego is one of my all-time favorites. He exuded charisma. If I was a horse, I think I might want to be Forego, but not a gelded Forego. If I was a racehorse, I'd want to go to stud.

In addition, it was a cumbersome 12-horse field, and Forego drew the 12-hole, the extreme outside post, which meant he was giving the field all sorts of lengths from the onset as he would be racing widest of all throughout. From where I sat in the Grandstand, it looked as if he was breaking from the parking lot.

Also adding to his woes, the Marlboro Cup was a Handicap and as he was clearly the best he was giving great gobs of weight to the field. As a general rule of thumb over a classic distance of a mile and a quarter, the distance at which the Marlboro Cup was run, every three pounds of weight given is thought to be worth a length, meaning that Forego, if my memory serves me correctly, was giving the second-high weight, Honest Pleasure, five lengths.

Further compromising Forego's chances, the second high-weight, Honest Pleasure, was a legitimate front runner, the only real early speed in the race, and he would most surely get loose on the lead without using himself much at all. And he did. At the ½ mile pole, Honest Pleasure was well clear, with scads of daylight between himself and the field. And he was going easily, having gotten the lead in effortless fashion, meaning that he would have that much more in reserve should anyone challenge.

Given the circumstances and the hurdles he had to overcome, if Forego had been defeated that day, his reputation would have lost little of its luster, as such a loss could be forgiven as he faced a plethora of legitimate excuses.

At one point, Forego was so far back, running on the extreme outside, that it appeared as if he had lost touch with the field.

Top of the stretch Honest Pleasure was five lengths to the good, still going easily. His rider looked back, sneaked a peek, and took note. I imagine at this point he was thinking about what exactly he was going to do with his share of the purse money: stocks, triple tax-free Munis, perhaps a new car, a down payment on a vacation home, etc.

Forego at the time was about ten or twelve lengths back, and it appeared that when the history of this race was written, he would be a mere footnote. I imagine if then and there I had asked anyone who had bet on Forego if they would take 50% on the dollar, they would have done so in a heartbeat.

But then, totally unexpected, Forego suddenly quickened and slowly, inexorably, commenced to accelerate with an uncommon suddenness that produced among those assembled a jaw-dropping awe as he morphed into something more akin to a speeding locomotive than a racehorse. The game was on. Forego was now a force of nature, as awesome and unstoppable as an avalanche. Slowly, inexorably, he ate into Honest Pleasure's lead. At the sixteenth pole, it appeared that no matter how gallant and stalwart an effort Forego was making, he would come up short, as he was simply running out of ground. Honest Pleasure's jockey felt Forego looming and took to the whip with great vigor. Honest Pleasure had a touch of class, and he responded in kind. It was clear he was not going to surrender without a fight.

But Forego, now transformed into an irresistible entity, just kept coming and coming and just did get up to beat Honest pleasure by a nose in what, in my opinion, was the signature race of his career. It was a most stirring exhibition as to what it means to be a real deal racehorse, as Forego overcame more adversity that day than most horses successfully deal with their entire career.

Shoemaker rode Forego that day. He was in awe. He said, "I never sat on a horse as determined," which is high praise indeed, as Willie Shoemaker has sat on a lot of good horses over the course of his long and fabled career. Willie the Shoe summed it up best when he said, "He would not be denied."

I dislike the word amazing. I try as best I can to avoid using the word because people use it without thought or reservation in any and all contexts. The word's meaning has been seriously degraded. When people don't seem to realize that if everything is amazing, nothing is. That being said, what Forego did that day was truly amazing.

A lesser sort might have used the loads of adversity that plagued Forego that day as an excuse. Excuses, though, are for losers, not for horses like Forego, class personified.

Much as I enjoy watching a highly competitive race and the drama that it brings to the table, from a betting point of view, I much prefer a race that is not all that competitive, provided, of course, the horse doing the routing is the horse I bet on. I like a horse, make a serious bet, I want my horse to have the field at his mercy. When I have skin in the game; I don't want drama, I want to cash tickets.

Winners

As per rule number four, the only way a horse can show me he is capable of accomplishing something is by doing it. As per this rule, I will not bet a horse to win until he has shown me he has 'winning ways'; and the only way a racehorse can do that is by winning races. The proof is in the pudding. As I only bet to win, this edict is non-negotiable. The only exception to any of my rules occurs if the Executive Racing Committee (The ERC) meets and grants a waiver. This rarely occurs. In fact, I can count on the fingers of one hand how many times such a waiver has been granted. I know all this because I happen to be the Chairman of the Executive Racing Committee. I'm also its only member. When it comes to the Executive Racing Committee, I have a great deal of influence. In fact, never, not once, has a decision of the Executive Racing Committee been overridden.

At the races, if you are unable to distinguish horses with 'winning ways' from those that lack them, you will end up enjoying the same level of success, or lack thereof, as a farmer who is unable to separate the wheat from the chaff. When you bet on a horse to win who lacks 'winning ways,' you are asking him to do something that's not part of his behavioral repertoire, like asking a duck not to waddle but to move instead with the shadowy grace of a cat. It's not going to happen.

Federico Tesio is considered the 20th century's most influential breeder. He bred Nearco, the penultimate foundation sire. In his book 'Training the Thoroughbred Racehorse,' Tesio says, "It is the things that you cannot see that are most important." The point being that for Tesio, a horse's mental conformation is as important, if not more so, than his physical attributes. When Tesio speaks of 'the things that you can't see,' he is referring to the two all-important intangibles: class and 'winning ways.'

I define a horse with 'winning ways' as a horse who not only wants to win but also knows how, two traits I want to see expressed before I will even consider investing in his or her chances. In other words, I will not bet on a horse to win unless he has convinced me that he or she understands the game, what constitutes victory, what does not, and expresses the necessary behaviors that must be engaged in, in order to accomplish that end, which we define as being first to breach the plane of the wire. A horse can run like the wind, have an abundance of stamina, and have a touch of class, but if he lacks 'winning ways,' he has as much chance of winning as a horse that is lame. It's like owning a Ferrari and not knowing how to drive.

I'm not saying that horses that lack 'winning ways' never win. They do. But it is an aberration. Aberrations are not to be counted on, as they are yet another subspecies of luck and impossible to foretell with any degree of accuracy.

Every race has a winner. If all the horses entered lack 'winning ways,' then a horse devoid of 'winning ways' has to win. Such a race comes to pass; it is more a commentary on the woefulness of the field than it is on the 'winning ways' of the horse who finds himself, perhaps much to his surprise, leading at the wire. Beating a bunch of Palookas, especially if the winner is a Palooka himself, is not a feather in a horse's cap. It counts for little. Before I will even toy with the idea that a thoroughbred has 'winning ways' and is the sort I might bet on, I will have had to see him take the measure of real-deal professionals who have already demonstrated to me, beyond equivocation, that they are in possession of 'winning ways.'

Not only do I want to know if a horse has 'winning ways' but I also want to have a handle on the depth and intensity of those desires. All things being equal, if three horses are abreast, 'hooked up,' battling at the 1/16th pole, and one of the horses wants to win, one really wants to win, and one of them really, really, really wants to win, I want my money on the latter of the three.

Horses with 'winning ways' can be found at all levels, from Grade I Stakes horses to bottom-of-the-barrel claimers running for $1,500 claiming tags at obscure venues. Basically, what determines the level at which a horse with 'winning ways' can win is the level at which he can dominate and impose his will, his class. If I think a horse has 'winning ways,' I'll bet him no matter the level he's racing at, provided I believe he's the class of the field, quite capable of bossing the others, competing on a course he likes, is in form, at a distance he can handle, and the pace won't overly degrade his chances. Some might say that these are quite a number of conditions that have to be met in order for me to bet on a horse. Correct. It is. I would rather make a lot of demands and win, than too few and lose.

I want to win and collect. I don't care how much I collect as long as I do not end up ripping up my tickets and throwing them away. I bet $2 on a horse that is 1–2, I get back $3.00. That's a 50% return on my investment in less than two minutes. The last time I looked, the banks were paying 2 ¾ %, and you had to keep your money deposited with them for at least a year. Call me old-fashioned, but if someone can explain to me how a 50% return on an investment in less than two minutes is a bad idea, I'd be interested. I'll take it all day, every day.

Having 'winning ways' is a highly valued trait that breeders hope can be passed from one generation to the next. Toward that end, prolific winners who showed great class are the ones that make their way to the breeding shed. A sire and dam that both exhibited 'winning ways' are far more likely to produce offspring with 'winning ways' than the progeny of thoroughbreds that were losers.

Which is why losers aren't bred. They're culled and either retired to pasture or turned into dog food. Expunging a loser's genetic material from the gene pool is one way of improving the breed.

As winners, not losers, have been rigorously selected to breed for the past several hundred years, it should come as no surprise that some horses are not only born with a strong, innate desire to win but also an understanding of how to do so. I do not mean to imply that thoroughbreds understand winning as we do. But clearly, there are horses who routinely engage in behavior the end product of which we would describe as winning, which I define yet again as being in control and leading at the wire.

Horses that are obsessive and compulsive in regards to winning are venerated and held in the highest regard, which is why they, not losers, contribute to the gene pool. Breeders want their products to win, not lose. All the best of the best, the top echelon, were monomaniacal when it came to winning. Thoroughbreds like Seattle Slew, Affirmed, Kelso, Secretariat, Dr. Fager, Ruffian, Buckpasser, Personal Ensign, American Pharoah, Zenyatta, et al., were all obsessed with being on the lead at the wire. It was their raison d'etre.

There is a reason why some horses win 16 of 62 lifetime starts and others win two of 43. The former have 'winning ways,' the latter do not. I cannot overstate the importance of a horse's mindset in this regard.

Res Ipsa Loquitor is Latin for 'things speak for themselves'. Anyone who doesn't believe that there are horses who really, really, really want to win should go to YouTube and watch Affirmed withstand Alydar in the final sixteenth of the Belmont Stakes, Personal Ensign run down Winning Colors in the Breeder's Cup, Forego collar Honest Pleasure at the wire in the '76 Marlboro Cup, or Seattle Slew come again to try and best Exceller in the Jockey Gold Cup.

To support my opinion that there are thoroughbreds who not only want to win but also know how to do so, I submit the following data points.

Waya ran in the mid-seventies. A turf filly, she shipped over from the Continent, France. At a classic distance on the turf, Waya was about as good as a mare gets. She had the intangibles in spades: 'winning ways' in abundance, as demonstrated by the fact that she rarely lost, and all sorts of class as she won more than her fair share of Grade I Stakes. For Waya, losing was anathema, something she simply would not abide. Her race in the Grade I Knickerbocker at Belmont, at a mile and a quarter on the turf, was, I think, her finest moment and speaks most aptly to the point I'm trying to make. Bowl Game, Macdermedia, and Tiller, to name but a few, all males, were entered as well. All were multiple Grade I Stakes winners. Bowl Game and Macdermedia were Eclipse Award winners. Though Tiller didn't have that credential on his resume, in my opinion, he was just as good as the two that did. In other words, the field the filly tried that day was brimming with quality.

I made a two-dollar bet on Tiller. He was a favorite of mine. I'd won a lot of races with him. He was a consummate, classy, hard-knocking professional who could get a classic distance of ground with ease, always tried his hardest, and when he 'fired,' kicked in, and quickened, could unleash a truly devastating turn of foot. I bet on him just for the sake of having a rooting interest. Also, I'm a loyal sort. In a field where all the horses have 'winning ways' and class to the nth degree and a legitimate case can be made for each and every one, it is best to keep one's hands in one's pocket. All you are really doing in such a circumstance is guessing and wishing, two modes of thought that make poor hinge points on which to base a wager. It was one of those very special races that come along every so often where you just sit back, enjoy, and savor the experience, like sipping a quality single malt scotch, neat, while sitting in front of the fireplace, indoors, warm and cozy on a cold, blustery, wintery evening.

Waya broke a tad slow, then eased her way to the rail and stayed glued there as the field rounded the clubhouse turn. She maintained her rail-hugging position, maybe 10 or so lengths behind the leaders, throughout the long run down Belmont's backstretch. Strategically, it was far from an ideal position. I kept waiting for Cordero Jr., her rider, to take her off the rail, so when she did make her run, finding racing room would not be an issue. I waited. She stayed where she was. I found it perplexing. Cordero Jr., Waya's rider, was a savvy sort. As the field made its way past the half-mile pole, Waya was still on the rail, still perhaps 10 lengths off the lead, her position now growing grossly untenable. She was pinned on the rail, trapped, boxed in, and surrounded on all sides by a picket fence of horse flesh. I thought her goose was cooked. At the time, I thought I would like to be privy to the conversation Waya's trainer would be having with Cordero Jr. afterward. Surely, there would be questions and recriminations. The French filly went like that around the turn, still stuck on the rail with no place to go. A friend of mine, standing next to me, had made a big bet on Waya. As the field turned into the stretch, he looked both crestfallen and nauseous. At this juncture, I assumed it just wasn't Waya's day, and that was that. It happens. What are you going to do? Racehorses aren't machines. They're only human. They have their off days. Also, even the best of riders can make a mistake. It is what it is.

As they straightened for home, a horse in front of Waya drifted out just a touch, a sliver of a gap appeared, and in the blink of an eye, Waya quickened and accelerated into the breach, found daylight, battled her way through, tapped into yet another gear, and took off after the leaders. 'A case of too little, too late' was the thought that came to mind. Now in full flight, an impressive sight, at the eighth pole, Waya reached the three horses strung out in front of her who were in steadfast pursuit of the horse on the lead two lengths in front of them. All were in high gear. Having wiggled free of one roadblock, Waya now encountered another. She slowed, nestled in behind the three for a jump or two, looked somewhat hesitant, as if appraising the situation, and then somewhat daintily stepped to the outside of the three, found her penultimate gear, and ran down the leader as if he'd been zapped and immobilized by a ray gun. She won going away in what could only be considered a most impressive performance.

Afterward, the commentator Frank Wright Jr. queried Cordero Jr. as to the ride, specifically his decision to stay on the rail. "Not me," Cordero Jr. answered. "She wanted the rail badly. A few times I tried to nudge her off, but she said no. I ask her again and again, but each time she says no. She's too good a filly to fight, so I say, okay, Momma, it's your race; take us home. She did what she wanted to do. I just went along for the ride."

Sounding like a proud father bragging about something his child had done, Cordero Jr. ended his analysis by saying, "She's one smart filly; she knew all along just what she wanted to do, and she did it." Certainly, Waya not only wanted to win but knew exactly how to do so.

Yet another example of what I am referring to. After Kelso and Forego, John Henry was the best gelding I ever saw. Once, when asked to explain what it was that made John Henry the winning force that he was, his trainer, Ron

McNally, said, "Not only does he really want to win, he knows how." He then explained how he had arrived at his opinion. "A horse changes leads; they have a tendency to accelerate for the next jump or two. Maybe it's because they're relieved to have the weight off the leg that was on the lead. I don't exactly know why. I just know that it happens. Whenever John Henry found himself in a head-to-head, in a tight spot, with the wire looming, he would change leads on his own, so that when it mattered most, he would have that extra little bit of oomph, which was the difference between his winning or coming second. It's something you can't teach. It's there or it is not. He was the only horse I ever trained who behaved that way. That's why," his trainer concluded, "John Henry didn't lose many bobs of the head. Never had a horse who wanted to win as much as that one did. Many races he impressed the heck out of me."

One summer that I worked, as a hot walker I got friendly with a trainer who was well into his eighties. He shared our barn. He walked with a cane. Wish I could remember his name, but I can't. It's been a while. He had four horses. He'd been on the backstretch his entire life. He knew nothing else. He was old enough so that he had trained horses when placing judges; not the electronic wizardry of photo-timers decided the order of finish. He told me about a horse he trained, a hard-knocking sort that won more than his fair share. One day the horse was involved in a close finish, and after much consultation and reflection, the judges placed the horse second. The colt, however, was of a different opinion, and in a matter-of-fact fashion, as if it were his right, he commenced making his way to the winner's circle. When his groom tried to dissuade him, the horse, usually a sensible, well-mannered sort, became unruly, and it was only with the utmost difficulty that they were able to lead him away, back to the barn. "Got me thinking," the old timer said. Next time out, he put the colt in with horses that he knew were better than the colt. As expected, the horse lost. After losing, he was led back to the barn without incident. The start after that, he put the colt in with cheaper, and as expected, the colt won. Prior to the race, the trainer had instructed the colt's groom that no matter the result, he was to lead the colt back to the barn, the same as if he had lost. The colt won. The groom attempted to do as he had been instructed, and the colt again displayed the same sort of truculence he'd exhibited the day that human frailty, as manifested by the placing judges, had placed him second.

"I will go to my grave," the old man concluded, "knowing in my heart of hearts that the day he was placed second, not only did he win, but he knew he won, and he was pissed that he wasn't awarded his due, that the judges had fucked up."

As noted earlier, the only way a horse can prove to me he has 'winning ways' is by winning. Would-haves and should-haves count for nothing. A horse breaks his maiden race and wins one race; to me, it doesn't make him a winner. All it means is that he won a maiden race against horses, none of whom have ever won. I wish I had a dollar for every horse that won a maiden race and never won again. Come to think of it, I wish I had a dollar for every horse that never even breaks his or her maiden and wins just once. If a horse wins a second or third race, all that means is that he has put two or three more notches on his belt. A horse cannot achieve professional, legitimate status, meaning he has convinced me he has 'winning ways,' until at minimum he has used up all his conditions and he wins a race in what I refer to as 'open' company, which I define as a race devoid of restrictions based on number of races won or where the horse was bred, as such races are populated with seasoned, proven winners who have already proven to me they have 'winning ways.'

A horse demonstrates that he has 'winning ways,' he gets on my radar. I then keep tabs on him. If the right situation comes along, I'll bet on him.

There is no rule that says a horse that has not used up his conditions cannot enter an 'open' race against veteran legitimate professionals. Think cannon fodder.

Also, it is not a good idea to bet winners of restricted, State Bred races to win in open company until they do so. Winning a State Bred $35,000 claimer is a lot, lot different than winning a $35,000 claiming race that sports no such restrictions.

Thoroughbreds who sport 'winning ways' as per my criteria are not as common as you might imagine. I just picked up Sunday's Racing Form. It contains the cards for Belmont, Santa Anita, Churchill Downs, Woodbine, Parx Racing, Laurel, Gulfstream, and Golden Gate.

In addition, Gulfstream is offering six races from Peru. I do not mean to cast aspersions on the integrity of the Peruvian racing community, but I imagine that having a working acquaintance with a Peruvian or two that knows the ins and outs of the Peruvian racing scene would be of great value when looking to cash a bet on a Peruvian horse race. I don't think I have ever met a Peruvian. There used to be a Peruvian place in the city. I ate there a few times. The food was good. The people who ran it, though, were Greek. That's as close as I have come to knowing a Peruvian.

There are a total of 84 races carded, with the Peruvian races not included. Only 14 of the 84 races are what I would categorize 'open' races.' All of the other races sport restrictive conditions of some sort. The 14 'open races' are the only races I will consider betting on, as they are the only races that contain professionals that can be relied on to win if given a suitable opportunity.

I most assuredly will not bet on any of the other 70 races in play for the simple reason that not one of the competitors comprising those fields have shown me, much less proved to me, as per my stipulations, that they have 'winning ways.'

All the data I have assembled over the years tells me that if I want to win, I can only bet on those 14 'open' races. I not only keep records; I also listen to what they have to say. If I didn't, my bank account would look as if it had gone through a paper shredder.

Another benefit of my only perusing the 14 races is that the fewer races I have to focus on, the better off I'll be, as I can process just so much information. Overloading is dangerous. Too much thinking, for me anyways, and the law of diminished returns kicks in. I know if I husband my mental energies and focus my cognitive energies on deciphering and deconstructing just those 14 races that are populated by horses with 'winning ways,' I have that much better chance of picking a winner than if I spread my brain power too thin by studying all 86 races. My cognitive energies are limited. It is important that I use them wisely.

If you can figure out who will win a race not populated with horses that have 'winning ways,' go for it. I have little or no idea how to do so. Therefore, I steer clear of such races.

Besides not betting on races where horses have yet to use up their conditions, I can't remember the last time I bet on a two-year-old. Their body of work is minimal; too meager a sample for me to extrapolate any meaningful understanding of what they can or cannot do. The same goes for races for three-year-old colts and fillies, as they too, to my mind at least, are still in the process of defining themselves.

Oftentimes, when I opt not to bet on a race because I believe none of the horses have 'winning ways,' I have been told by my cohorts, 'but every race has a winner.' No argument here; there will be a winner. The issue is, how does one go about picking the winner from a field where it appears that none of the entrants care all that much if they win or lose? To me, betting in such circumstances is akin to playing a game of pure chance. If that's the way I want to go, I'll buy lottery tickets or go to a casino and play the slot machines.

Usually, a horse doesn't get on my radar, if indeed he does, till late in his three-year-old campaign. Most of the horses I bet for the first time usually have at least nine to ten races under their belt. I mean, there are exceptions, but they are few and far between.

Come to think of it, I just remembered an instance where I decided that it was okay to bet on a two-year-old. After Seattle Slew's third race as a two-year-old, when he laid waste to the field at a mile in the Grade I Champagne Stakes, I instinctively knew he was special, unique, and a true outlier in the most positive sense. I met with the Executive Racing Committee, (The ERC), a vote was taken, and it was decided unanimously then and there that I could bet Seattle Slew despite him being a two-year-old. Seattle Slew didn't run again as a two-year-old but I bet him his first race back as a three-year-old and then forever after. I'm a big fan of Seattle Slew. He was special and then some.

Losers are not on my radar. What for? Why waste my time, energy, and emotions contemplating horses that I'm never going to bet on?

The number of races a horse wins is not the only metric I use to determine if a horse has 'winning ways.' The percentage of wins is a meaningful indicator as well. Six wins in 16 starts make a far more robust statement as to the chances a horse might indeed have 'winning ways' than if it takes a horse 63 races to register his fifth win.

In regards to winning, certain behavior catches my eye. When I see a horse overcome adversity to win, whatever it may be, it gets my attention, as it tells me in no uncertain terms that he's focused on winning and won't be dissuaded.

I also give special props to horses who win the close ones. A horse battles, ding dongs it with another horse the length of the stretch, and wins a photo by a nostril he's telling me he really, really understands the game and really wants to win. Winning by a nose tells me more about a horse's desire to win than when a horse simply draws off and wins for fun by half the length of the stretch.

An even more zealous testament, as previously noted, as to a horse's desire to win is when he or she comes again. A horse comes again; he's making quite the statement as to his desire to prevail.

Losers

Knowing which horses lack 'winning ways' is as important, if not more so, than knowing which horses have them. If one cannot distinguish a winner from a loser, the chances of enhancing one's bankroll are about the same as those of a prospector who cannot tell fool's gold from the real thing.

Identifying losers is a critical yet unappreciated skill. Though it lacks the glamor and panache associated with selecting a winner, seeing a loser for the loser that he or she is adds all sorts of value as it keeps one from investing in a horse whose chances are dubious at best. It's addition by subtraction. Of further benefit, by identifying and eliminating losers, it makes it that much easier for the winners to come to light, allowing them to self-identify, as if they were crystals precipitating out of a solution.

The most egregious losers are the 'dead pieces.' Post-race comments describe their performance as 'never a factor,' 'trailed throughout,' 'no threat,' 'showed nothing,' 'did little, etc. If you can't identify the 'dead pieces,' I suggest you stay home. 'Dead pieces' appear to have no skin in the game and couldn't care less if they win or lose. 'Dead pieces' go through the motions. They show up. They run. But have no real impact on the proceedings. It appears that rather than race, they would much prefer to be in their stalls munching hay, hanging out, and shooting the breeze with their stablemates. I imagine people refer to such horses as 'dead pieces' because they show little life.

This is not to say a 'dead piece' never wins. They do. It happens. It is irksome, to say the least. A 'dead piece' awakes from his torpor runs a big race; it can leave me slack-jawed with shock. Same as what would happen if I witnessed a cadaver clamber up out of his grave and commence to skip rope. For me, there are no discernible patterns or clues that will portend a 'dead piece' winning. My chances of predicting when a 'dead piece' will win are on par with a ship's Captain predicting when and where a rogue wave will arise from the deep and send him, his vessel, and his crew to a watery grave. A 'dead piece' wins, all I can do is scratch my head and wonder what it all means, like nighttime when I lie awake in bed, awaiting sleep, alone with my thoughts, and I find myself contemplating the vastness of a night time sky as it twinkles with starlight outside my window.

A professional sort beats the horse I thought best, I tip my hat to him. A 'dead piece' beats me; I have been known to become irritable. When such an occurrence comes to pass, rather than say or do something, I might later regret, it. I go off and sit by myself, where I quietly smolder until my annoyance and frustration lessens to the point where I can once again mingle with others and I am able to spout with ease all the empty chit-chat and bromides that help get us through the day.

If a professional sort gets beat by a random unknowable, such as a 'dead piece,' it is a legitimate excuse.

A 'dead piece' wins; next race, I will keep an eye on him. Some horses, like people, are late bloomers. Sometimes a 'dead piece' evolves into a professional. Nine times out of ten, though, no such transformation occurs, and next race the 'dead piece' runs, he performs once again like the 'dead piece' he is.

Being beaten by a 'dead piece' is one thing. Betting on a 'dead piece' and losing is another. It is an inexcusable, unforced error. Anyone who bets on a 'dead piece', they deserve to lose. If you wager on one too many 'dead pieces,' you will end up as a 'stooper.' Someone constantly attempts to make cases for a 'dead piece' winning; chances are he was dropped on his head as a baby one too many times.

Usually, a race can be a teachable moment. Something new is learned. There is a morsel of knowledge and a nugget of insight to be gained. Not so when a 'dead piece' wins. A 'dead piece' wins, afterward, no matter how fine a comb I use to parse the event and stretch my imagination, I can come up with no other explanation than 'shit happens.' In order for me to find a rationale to make sense of such an occurrence, I'd have to push the envelope of my reasoning far beyond its breaking point.

The only time I expect a 'dead piece' to win is when the entire field is composed of 'dead pieces.' If all the horses are 'dead pieces,' a 'dead piece' has to win. Don't expect me to tell you which 'dead piece.' That's a separate issue. I just know the winner is going to be a 'dead piece.' Trying to seek a winner in such a field is not a good idea, unless, of course, you fancy yourself a good guesser.

The cheaper the race, the more likely it is that it will be filled with 'dead pieces.' 'Dead pieces' don't compete in, much less win races with large purses for the simple reason that they don't belong and have no chance.

An excellent opportunity to make a serious bet arises when one is lucky enough to come upon a field composed of 'dead pieces,' save one, a professional, who by definition has 'winning ways.' Such situations are rare. When I stumble upon such a scenario, I imagine I feel the same way a thirst-stricken desert traveler feels upon seeing before him a lush, watery oasis that he knows is not a mirage, having stopped there and refreshed himself when traveling with previous caravans.

I have no problem making a serious bet on a $5,000 claimer if he is a legitimate sort, in form, at a distance he likes, on a surface he relishes, and the others entered are all 'dead pieces' save him. In fact, I relish the opportunity. If only I could come across a wizard who could teach me an incantation that could make such situations a far more common occurrence.

When a 'dead piece' wins, the payout, for good reasons, can be huge. When a horse wins at long odds, he is said to pay 'boxcars.' Why 'boxcars?' I have no idea. Maybe it's because when a long shot wins, the numbers indicating the winning payouts take up lots of space on the tote board, same as a fleet of boxcars take up lots of space when they're parked off to the side on a railway siding. Unlike myself, there are players whose game is all about looking to cash in on horses that pay 'box cars.' Such players often make wagers on horses I consider 'dead pieces.' Horses that I wouldn't bet with counterfeit money. People who look to score 'box cars' have a unique ability to make a case for practically any horse, no matter how woeful his history.

They have a surfeit of imagination. Such players can come up with multiple reasons why a 'dead piece' can win, no matter how abysmal horse's career and current form. They do so with little effort, easy as a magician pulling a rabbit out of a hat. I know people who, in the blink of an eye, can come up with a litany of reasons that they would deem creditable as to why a horse with three legs should be seriously considered. 'Box car' guys don't often smile; they're a stoic lot. But when they do, they have ear-to-ear shit-eating grins.

Horse players tend to recollect their 'scores' more readily than they do their losses. This is especially true for those seeking 'boxcar' like 'scores.' In my experience, such individuals tend to forget the losses they suffered, just as a trauma victim is often unable to recollect the accident that put him in intensive care. One thing I will say about those who seek 'box cars,' they have patience in abundance. Also, they are usually plagued with cash flow problems.

I know a 'boxcar' guy that cashes 'boxcar' bets more often than most 'boxcar' guys do. Still, overall, he's a loser. I've known him for years. He has his reasons for doing what he does, but they make no sense. Not to me at least. He is not all that bright or well rounded. He claims 'reading will make you stupid.' Once, for some reason, we got into a discussion of the solar system. He steadfastly maintained that April was the planet furthest from the sun after Mars. Apparently he confused Mars with the month of March. Also, he thinks that when someone is debriefed, they are asked to take off their underwear. Once he bragged to me that he was fluent in prose. But I give him credit. He does have access to some strand of reasoning that allows him every so often to cash 'box car' tickets on 'dead pieces,' which I wouldn't bet on with make-believe money. Trust me, I've tried to learn from him, but I can't, as we seem to dwell in starkly different realities. He's one of a kind. Also, he's a nice guy and good company, and I wish him the best. I have already assured him I will come to visit him on a regular basis when the men in white coats eventually come, as they most certainly must, to take him away. Come to think of it, I haven't seen him in a while.

Throwing out an egregious loser like a 'dead piece' is relatively easy. 'Dead pieces' are pretty upfront as to their woefulness. Their ineptitude is obvious even to the most myopic. 'Dead pieces' are honest and upfront as to their shortcomings. I respect them for their forthrightness. They are far different than those losers that one must be especially wary of, as the manner in which they lose is somewhat disingenuous. Their performances' dissemble. Like wolves in sheep's clothing, they misrepresent themselves. Their efforts mislead and tend to leave the impression that they are winners, when in fact they are anything but. Surely, they don't intend to mislead; there is no malice involved; it is simply a matter of how they go about their business. They are what they are. They mean you no harm. Bet on such a loser; it's on you. Same as if you picked up a venomous snake you thought harmless.

What characterizes such horses is that no matter how hard they seem to try, no matter how well positioned, or how favorable the circumstances, they never do close the deal and win. They are 'live pieces.' They make impressive-looking runs, appear ardent, but are always a day late and a dollar short, and lose in such a manner, by a nose, a half head, a neck, that they bait you into thinking that next time out, surely, they will win. But the fact of the matter is that their chances of winning are the same as a 'dead piece.' But because of the manner in which they lose, they conjure up the illusion that they have the potential to actually win.

Horses that are especially adept at seducing you into thinking that they are winners when they are anything but are known as 'money burners.' The reason for this appellation is because the chances of enhancing one's bankroll by betting on a 'money burner' are about the same as increasing one's net worth by throwing hundred-dollar bills into a furnace. Alchemists of a sort, 'money burners,' are adept at not only transmuting paper money into ash but also hope into despair.

Knowing a horse is a 'money burner' is invaluable. Not only will you save money by not betting on him, but you will also learn to love him or her in a perverse sort of way, as they are great to bet against. Over bet as they usually are, they create underlays. This means the others in the field have to be, to one degree or the other, overlays. An underlay occurs when the money bet on a horse to win is disproportionate to his actual chances of winning, or at least in my opinion. If I like a horse, the more 'money burners' populate the field, the happier I am. If, because of the presence of a 'money burner' or two, I get three to one on a horse I think should be 3–5 my eyes might well mist over with unalloyed joy. Granted, underlays and overlays are in the eyes of the beholder. This is okay with me. I believe I am more rooted in what's real and what's not, than most.

I much prefer a horse that I like to be an overlay, but should I like such a horse, I'll bet on him even if he is an underlay and accept it for what it is: yet another unfortunate thread that every so often weaves its way into the fabric of my life.

Occasionally a 'money burner' beats me, just as I sometimes get beat by a 'dead piece.' I will say this, though: without a doubt, over the years I have made a lot more money betting against 'money burners' than I have made betting on them.

A front-running 'money burner' is known as a 'quitting rat.' A 'money burner' that comes from off the pace is referred to as a 'hanging dog.' 'Rats' and 'dogs' are easy to spot. When push comes to shove, with the race on the line, and they are 'hooked up,' head to head, battling for the lead, they inevitably surrender, wilt, retire from the fray, give in, and allow the horse or horses testing them to put their heads in front and assume control. Though they might put on a good show and appear to be in the thick of things with real chances of winning, they never do grasp the brass ring. As inevitable as fate itself, they eventually assume a subordinate position. 'Rats' and 'dogs' lack will, resolve, and gumption, to name but a few of their shortcomings. They say 'Uncle,' sometimes grudgingly so, but in the end they always do. For them, succumbing is a way of life.

I have no respect for 'rats' and 'dogs.' They have no heart and little class. They get bullied. They look for reasons to lose, not win. In terms of how one should conduct oneself on one's journey through life, they are the antithesis of proper role models.

The more ardent a 'rat's' or a 'dog's 'performance, the more likely it is that he will fool you. 'Rats' that spit out the bit at the eighth pole and go backward as if shot are easy to spot. It's the ones that battle willingly to the end only to lose by a bob of the head that are the most nefarious and insidious sort, as they are that much more adept at weaving their spider's web of deception.

The only time a 'rat' or a 'dog' wins, it's because he or she is in a field composed of not only 'dead pieces' but 'rats' and 'dogs' that are bigger 'rats' and 'dogs' than they are. A 'rat' or a 'dog' beats a 'rat' or a 'dog,' I don't get excited. A 'rat' or a 'dog' beats a professional sort fair and square, I take note. Perhaps he is evolving. For the most part, though, 'rats' and 'dogs,' like leopards and their spots, rarely change. Next race, they will be back to being who and what they are.

When a 'rat' or a 'dog' gives way, as is their want, they are said to have 'ratted out.' One of the reasons they are as successful at getting people to throw good money after bad is that they are adept at generating a plethora of 'what ifs.' What if he had moved earlier or later? What if the race was longer or shorter? What if he wasn't on the rail or stuck on the outside, or the inside, and so on and so forth, all 'what ifs.' I much prefer to deal with what is rather than what if. The more 'what ifs' a 'rat' or 'dog' produces, the subtler and more convincing they are, the more likely it is that they will inveigh their apologists to throw more good money after bad the next time he or she runs in a vain attempt to make up for the losses that have already been inflicted.

A 'what if' is an illegitimate excuse, a spurious concoction; it is the antithesis of a legitimate excuse. A legitimate excuse adds to one's knowledge and understanding of a horse in a positive and productive fashion. A 'what if' adds nothing. A 'rat' or a 'dog' loses a closely run affair, 'what ifs' inevitably materialize, often in abundance. Apparently, a 'what if' makes it that much easier for an individual who has made an errant bet on a loser to assuage his ego. A 'what if' offers solace. It's like a condolence card. It's much easier and more comforting to convince oneself into believing they were victimized by a 'what if' than to realize that their opinion might not be as crisp and prescient as they think. Given the choice between confronting themselves with discomforting realities, people often opt to pull the wool over their own eyes. The more of one's ego is invested in one's opinion, the less likely it is they will be able to look at what transpired with a cool, jaundice-free eye. For some, finding fault with themselves is unpalatable. It is much easier to put the blame elsewhere. 'Rats' and 'dogs' do not help people put their best foot forward.

While perhaps being overzealous in patting myself on the back, I think one of my strengths as a horse player is that I'm tough on myself. If I make a mistake, I take ownership.

Quite often I see people bet on a 'rat,' and then when the 'rat' rats out, rather than see the horse as the money-burning 'rat' that he is, they come up with a 'what if,' and next time the 'rat' runs, they double down on his chances. It becomes a vicious cycle. Stick with a 'rat' long enough, you will tap out. It's like death from a thousand cuts. If you're looking for a 'rat' to win and, in so doing, validate all the 'what ifs' you have come up with to excuse his previous losses, no good will come out of it.

A brief digression. Talk about negative, counterproductive emotions that have no place at the racetrack. I know people who wage vendettas against horses that beat them fair and square. A horse beats the horse they bet on, they take it as an insult, an act of disrespect. They then try to exact revenge by betting against the horse that beat them. Tit for tat has no place at the races. It's just plain childish and dumb. When someone makes a bet solely motivated by revenge, it's called a 'grudge bet.' When someone loses such a bet, I see it as justice being done, a fool getting his just dessert. When someone holds a grudge against a horse, I think they are working something out with either their mother or father that was never fully resolved.

I used to hang out with a guy who hated Buckpasser, because Buckpasser kept beating him. So in order to get even and teach Buckpasser a lesson, so to speak, he kept betting against Buckpasser. He lost a lot of money. The man wasn't stupid. Perhaps emotionally stunted, but not dumb. To this day, I cannot fathom why he didn't understand that Buckpasser, when sound, was about as good as a racehorse gets and that betting against him had the same sort of result as taking a firecracker, lighting it, sticking it up your nose, and expecting a positive result.

Even though 'rats' and 'dogs' are not going to win, one still has to pay attention to them. 'Rats' are 'live pieces,' meaning they will bring their speed into play and make a run. 'Dead pieces' do not. When and where a horse uses his speed, even if he is not going to win, is one of the dynamics that dictate the pace. One can't figure out the pace with any degree of proficiency if one has no inkling as to when and where horses will use their speed. This includes 'rats' and 'dogs.'

When a 'rat' is passed and put away, he never ever attempts to 'come again' and retake the lead.

When a 'rat' is a front-runner, he attempts to lead from start to finish. Toward this end, he brings his speed into play from the onset. The only way such a 'rat' will win is if no other horse 'hooks' him, or whatever horses do engage him are bigger 'rats' than he is, or the track bias is so overwhelmingly in his favor that he cannot help but win.

A 'rat' on the lead will have the lead until he is 'hooked' by a professional, a winner, who seeks to assert his dominance. It might be soon after they break, somewhat later on, but whenever it occurs, the 'rat' will eventually give way. He might battle a touch, maybe a little more than a touch, but sooner or later, he gives in. The thing about a 'rat,' no matter how slow the pace or how much advantage he accrues because of it, when challenged in earnest, though he might offer a bit of a tussle, he will inevitably 'rat out' and assume a subordinate position.

When horses are bobbing heads, it's the 'rat's' head that is always a bob behind. 'Rats' do not win photos.

A professional frontrunner is 'hooked' and gives way, there might well be something to be learned. Like he was not as classy as I thought he was. He didn't like the distance or the racing surface, or the pace compromised his chances, etc. One salvages what one can from the defeat. Hopefully, something is learned. When a 'rat' 'rats out,' there is nothing to be learned because that's what 'rats' do. A 'rat' cannot have a legitimate excuse.

'Rats' that 'rat out' coming from off the pace are known as 'hanging dogs.' They are referred to as such because, come crunch time, in the midst of their challenge, no matter how fierce and inexorable their run, upon reaching and 'hooking' the leader, as soon as they are met with any semblance of resistance, their challenge is withstood. They never do take control. They seem to hang, as if snagged on something.

'Hanging dogs' can be visually impressive. They fire, loom boldly, and look as if they are going to inhale the leader as easily as sucking down an oyster, but they are inevitably repulsed and 'put away.' The more impressive a 'hanging dog' runs, the more likely it is that he will fool people into thinking that he really was a threat, and the horse on the lead was indeed in jeopardy. 'Hanging dogs' are as good, if not better, at generating 'what ifs' than 'quitting rats.' A 'hanging dog' hangs the usually 'what if' is the jockey. The other day I saw a 'hanging dog' 'hang' like the rat he is. The guy next to me says, "Jockey fucked up, moved too soon." The guy sitting on my other side says, "Jockey fucked up; he moved too late." What they don't seem to get is that the horse is a 'hanging dog' and is going to hang no matter when and where he makes his move. That's the key.

The most convincing testimony that a closer is a 'hanging dog' occurs when there aren't any what-ifs that hold water. Like there is a speed duel up front that saps the pace setters' energies, and the 'hanging rat' sits the 'garden trip.' Yet still, when he makes his move, looms threateningly, and reaches his foes, all of whom are clearly leg weary and staggering, going backward and decelerating, he still lacks the will to get by and gain control. Still, even then, people find excuses. Apparently, there is an inexhaustible treasure trove of 'what ifs' frolicking in the zeitgeist that people can tap into to cover any contingency to explain away their stupidity.

'Hanging dogs' come in lots of shapes: some stalk, sitting just beyond the pacesetter; some came from mid-pack; others from way back; and still others from the 'clouds,' which is to say so far back that they appear to have fallen out of touch. But still, no matter from where they commence their run or how emphatic their move is, they hang like the 'hanging dogs' they are.

How do I know when a horse is 'ratting out,' and it is not just a matter of his or her being beaten fair and square? Remember what Supreme Court Justice Stewart said about pornography, "Though I can't define it, I know it when I see it." It's the same for me when it comes to spotting a 'rat.' I simply know a 'rat' when I see one. It's a gift.

A 'rat' classic occurs when a 'hanging dog' hooks a quitting 'rat.' Perhaps not as dramatic as when an irresistible force meets an immovable object, but interesting nonetheless. It's the same paradox, only backward; the issue being what transpires when an eminently movable object meets a dissolute force.

****

An especially insidious species of 'money burner' are those horses afflicted, as if by disease, by an ability to come in second no matter the circumstance. When a horse repeatedly comes second, it stirs up a veritable sandstorm of 'what ifs,' which tend to obscure the obvious, and that is, the horse in question has 'seconditis.' Coming second lends itself to making excuses and generates a plethora of 'what ifs.' It is far easier to come up with a credible excuse for a horse that comes in second by half a head than a horse that finished ninth, twenty lengths back. But alas and alack, it doesn't really matter how viable the 'what if' is for a horse with 'seconditis.' The reason the horse came second is because he has 'seconditis,' case closed.

Sometimes it appears as if horses with 'seconditis' are playing a different game, where coming second rather than winning is what it is all about. Breeding horses is not a science. The process can and will produce undesirable traits, outliers. Coming in second falls into that category. I've seen horses with 'seconditis' that had real talent. Unfortunately, they wanted to come in second, not win. A horse comes second race after race, he's not telling me he is on the cusp of winning; rather, the message is quite the opposite; he's telling me in no uncertain terms that as far as he is concerned, coming second is a fine and dandy outcome.

One doesn't have to be especially intuitive to discern a horse with 'seconditis.' Simply look at his record. A horse that has run 42 times, won three races, placed 12 times, and come third on eight occasions clearly has 'seconditis.' A sure sign that a horse has 'seconditis' is if his connections, in search of a victory, commence dropping him down into softer and softer spots and he still comes second. Drop-downs with 'seconditis' can burn their way through scads of money, easy as a hot knife through margarine. People who lose on a horse with 'seconditis' often fall into the trap of continuing to bet on them in the hope that they will eventually get even via a drop-down. Big mistake. Looking for the irredeemable to supply you with redemption is not a good idea.

I find horses with 'seconditis' to be a most nefarious sort of 'money burner.' People get attached to and emotionally vested in such horses. Horses with seconditis are especially good at getting people to throw good money after bad. Let's say the last two times you bet on a horse, he came in second. You are starting to have doubts. But you're caught in the horns of a dilemma. How stupid will you feel if you don't bet the horse his next time out, and he not only wins, he beats the horse that you bet on to beat him. After a while, betting such horses becomes like taking out an insurance policy to keep oneself from taking the bitter pill they might have to swallow the day you don't bet the horse and he wins.

Horses with 'seconditis' tease the fans the same as 'quitting dogs' and 'hanging rats.' They make strong, forceful, oftentimes eye-opening moves. They are definitely a presence; they battle; they give off a palpable sense of intensity and appear as if they are most certainly in the thick of things with as good a chance as any other, but it is always the same, and victory, which appears well within their grasp, always remains tantalizingly out of reach.

Horses with seconditis can be useful horses. They earn their keep and pay their way. They just don't win. There was a horse in the early eighties. His name eludes me. He came second, I think, in at least 12 races in a row. He was tough as hickory and ran every week or 10 days, always with the same result: second. Didn't matter who he ran against; he came in second. And always in more or less the same fashion. He'd stalk, make a big move as the field turned for home, catch, 'hook,' put the leader away, and secure the lead. And then, after putting the leader away, he would pull up and let another horse get past, only one, mind you, whereupon he'd fight like a demon to hold second.

What astounded me and still boggles my mind to this day, despite the fact he ran second in every race, week after week, he was always heavily bet to win. Lots of times, he was the favorite. Once or twice, he was odds on. I could understand betting him to place because that's what he did. But betting on him to win, I didn't get it. It was like he was the leader of a cult that had talked his followers into drinking Kool-Aid. If there was a Hall of Fame for 'money burners,' he would get in on the first ballot with nary a dissenting vote.

Interestingly enough, supporting my belief that he was genetically hardwired to seek second, he had a half-brother who raced in the exact same manner, earlier, in the mid-seventies. The half-brother was a watershed for me. He taught me everything I needed to know about the ability of a horse with seconditis to play havoc with my hopes and dreams, as well as my cash flow. I learned from the suffering he inflicted. It was a unique tutorial.

I personally have nothing against horses with 'seconditis.' In fact, I love them. They are great to bet against as they are always heavily bet out of all proportion to their chances, yet have no chance of winning. I like a horses' chances, how can I not be filled with joy when I see a horse with 'seconditis' entered in the same race? They suck up all sorts of undeserved money, and the horse I like becomes an overlay. When this happens, I lick my lips in anticipation, same as if I were a fat person about to be seated at an all-you-can-eat buffet.

Another type of 'money burner' is the 'excuse horse.' The 'excuse horse' is the personification of 'what ifs.' There is such a thing as a legitimate excuse. But for some horses, excuses are a way of life. If, race after race, something untoward befalls a horse and they are constantly besieged by bad fortune, I commence to question their racing competence. When a horse is always either forced wide, blocked, clipping heels, getting left at the gate, moving too early or too late, is disqualified, etc., what he or she is telling me is that they are not a victim, but rather that they don't really understand the game and how it should be played. If they did have a clue as to the point of the ritual, to win and, in so doing, display their dominance, they would go about their business differently. A legitimate, professional sort doesn't find trouble; he avoids it. Why? He understands. He gets it. He has a clue.

****

Another sort of money burner is the 'morning glory.' In their morning works, 'morning glories' put in blistering fast works which seduce the untutored, who are consumed with 'numbers' that the horse is sitting on ready and primed for a big race. However, even though when the dew glistens in the AM, and such horses run holes in the wind, come the afternoon, when it is time to race, they run, but don't win. Their physical talents are rendered moot as they lack either 'winning ways,' a modicum of class, or both. No matter how blessed a horse might be in terms of athletic talent, he will not win unless he knows and understands the game and

90

wishes to dominate and impose his will. Again, horses compete not to see who is fastest, but who is best.

****

I would be remiss in my discussion of excuses if I did not address the issue of the jockey as scapegoat. I'm not saying jockeys don't make mistakes. They do. They're human. But in no way do they deserve the amount of blame and calumny that is heaped upon them race after race. A jockey can make a difference and impact things both positively and negatively, but in my opinion, most of the time, a jockey is only as good as the horse he's on. I've yet to see a jockey leap off his mount at the sixteenth pole, sling said mount over his shoulder, and carry him to victory. Nine times out of ten, at minimum, if one really wants to understand why the horse he bet on lost, one would be better served focusing on the horse's performance, not the jockey.

****

Another excuse that I constantly encounter is that the races are fixed. I find pinning a loss on some secretive cabal that conspires to control outcomes silly to the extreme and a decidedly unproductive way of looking at things. First off, if you think the outcome is fixed, the race a fraudulent exercise, and you still bet, then you have a few screws loose, unless, of course, you like being cheated and relish victimhood. Humans are corrupt. To think that any of our institutions, of which horse racing is one, would be completely free of skullduggery would be naïve. But if you

91

truly believe that it is an integral part of the game and the majority of races are fixed, all I have to say to such people, if you have any proof as to such ongoing collusion and corruption, please come forward. I will be the first to help launch an investigation.

****

There is such a thing as a legitimate excuse. If something untoward happens to a professional that keeps him from running his or her race, much less winning, it is a legitimate excuse. When a professional has a legitimate excuse, there is a silver lining. Next time out, if people fail to realize the horse had a legitimate excuse and also that the variable that supplied the excuse is not in play in his upcoming race, an overlay may well be in the offing.

For example, the last time a horse ran, it was at a mile. The horse doesn't like a mile. A horse doesn't care for distance; it is a legitimate excuse. Today he's back at six furlongs, his specialty. Those that ascribe his loss at a mile to the pace, or his form, or whatever, and not to the real reason, the mile distance, will be foregoing an excellent opportunity to perhaps cash a winning bet by leveraging a legitimate excuse.

If a legitimate horse has a legitimate excuse, I much prefer that he finish way up the track rather than lose by a nose, as the further back he finishes, the darker his form, the more lackluster his effort will appear. A horse has a legitimate excuse. I want his performance to appear as abysmal as possible so that next time out, people give his chances the same lack of consideration I would accord a 'dead piece.'

Only a professional, legitimate sort of horse can have a legitimate excuse. 'Quitting rats,' 'hanging dogs,' 'excuse horses,' horses with seconditis, etc. cannot. They lose because they are losers.

Sometimes the answer as to why the horse I bet on lost is simple: my opinion was defective. I picked the wrong horse. Though I am always on the alert for a legitimate excuse, I will not force the issue because doing so could cause me to concoct a spurious 'what if.' If I lose because my opinion was wrong, it is much better for me to feel the pain the loss inflicts. That way, I am that much less likely to make the same mistake again.

Moves

A horse's moves are his gears; the notches he can let out. The faster, the longer, the more intense a move, the more potent it is. When a horse makes a move, he accelerates and picks up the pace. There's a strong correlation between a horse's moves, especially his best move, and the level at which he can compete.

A horse can have awesome moves and accelerate as if jet-propelled, but again, and I cannot overstate this, if he lacks the intangibles, 'winning ways' and 'class,' his moves will be of little to no pertinence. A horse has awesome moves and the athletic ability to run a hole in the wind, but little to no class; it is like a dog that is all bark and no bite. Class, a horse's relative ability to impose his will upon the other is what gives a thoroughbred's moves their integrity, resolve, and the requisite grit and backbone needed for them to have an impact.

A racehorse is like an oarsman, and a horse race is not unlike a regatta. In both, the participants brandish pace as if it were a cudgel. When a horse makes a move, accelerates, and picks up the beat, he sends a message to his rivals, same as when a coxswain calls upon his oarsmen to quicken the cadence. In both cases, the message to the competition is the same: ante up or suffer defeat. Oarsmen 'hook up,' same as horses.

A horse's moves, like an oarsman's paces, are like the arsenal of punches a prizefighter has at his disposal. They are bits and pieces of adversity that can be brought to bear on an opponent in an attempt to weaken, defy, and subjugate. Same as a strong left hook can send an opponent crashing to the canvas, dissuading and discouraging him from continuing, a particularly awesome move can intimidate, demoralize, and cause a horse to crack and concede.

Of all a horse's moves, the one I want to be most conversant with is his best move. A horse's best move is analogous to a prizefighter's best punch or a pitcher's best pitch. It is critical to be conversant with it, as it is the strongest, most emphatic statement a horse can make on his behalf. If a horse's best move is absent or not the least bit up to par, his chances of winning, no matter how stalwart his intangibles, are severely compromised, the same as it is tough for a pitcher to win, no matter how determined he is, if his fastball lacks that extra little bit of zip and his curveball is hanging like a 'hanging dog.'

A horse's best move is referred to as his 'speed.' When a horse shows his 'speed,' he is said to sport his 'brilliance.' When a horse's best move is brought into play, he attains his maximum velocity. Most horses can sustain their speed, their maximum velocity, whatever it might be, for about a quarter of a mile. This is most important.

At the races, as in any aspect of life, or so I have learned, there is no such thing as a free lunch. Everything is a tradeoff. In terms of the energy that will be left at his disposal, a racehorse pays an onerous price for the use of his speed after it has been brought into play. The amount of energy needed to fund his best move, that critical quarter mile where he flaunts his top gear, his most imposing move, takes so much out of him that after that quarter mile or so run has been made, a horse's energies are so depleted that he is no longer able to accelerate in any meaningful fashion and he is said to be 'used-up.' Not only can a 'used up' horse no longer accelerate, but the pool of energy from which he draws his vigor are now so critically depleted that he commences to decelerate. Having elided into deceleration mode, no longer able to accelerate, a thoroughbred lacks the wherewithal to either challenge for, or defend a lead. A 'used-up' racehorse is like a prizefighter who has punched himself out.

I cannot overestimate the importance of understanding the dynamic between a horse's speed and the toll it takes on his energies, and with it his ability to accelerate. Being able to understand and parse this critical concept, as simple as it may seem, is a must if one hopes to apprehend, appreciate, and make sense of the manner in which the pace of a race impacts its participants.

A horse's speed is put to its best use, either defending or acquiring the lead. Once his best move is brought into play, the 'speed' card played, if after a quarter of a mile, the lead has not been acquired or successfully defended, a horse's chances of winning recede accordingly, and whatever grip he might have had on winning, getting the job done and taken hold of the brass ring, begins to slip from his grasp. A horse brings his 'speed' into play; it creates a window of opportunity that he had best put to good advantage.

Unlike a prize fighter's best punch, a horse's 'speed'; cannot be used over and over again. In the best case scenario, when a horse brings his speed into play, it is the coup de grace. He uses it to put the field away and end any and all questions as to who is best.

If all the horses in the field are 'used up,' decelerating to one degree or another, a decelerating horse will win. The question of which horse will win is then ironically decided by which horse is going least slowly.

A 'used up' horse on the lead, one who has fired his best shot and is decelerating, can still win if the horses behind him, though accelerating, are not going quickly and deftly enough to make up the ground needed to reach and get past him before he reaches the finish line. In such a case, a decelerating horse on the lead wins, it's like a prizefighter being saved by the bell.

Horses that either lack any meaningful burst of speed or, for whatever reason, have it but deign not to use it are 'dead pieces.' When a horse brings his speed into play, he is said to 'fire.' If a horse doesn't 'fire,' he is said to have come up 'empty.' Coming up 'empty' is the principle attribute that defines a 'dead piece.'

If a professional who routinely 'fires' comes up empty and never shows his 'speed,' it is important to investigate why, which means figuring out what was the key to explain what transpired. The answer might well involve a legitimate excuse. If so, next time out, if the excuse is no longer in play, such a horse might well fashion a win at an overlay.

If I am unable to come up with a reason, a key, to explain why a horse didn't fire, I take a wait-and-see approach. I will not bet on him again until he demonstrates he is once again in possession of his speed and is more than willing to deploy it.

Seeing moves is simply an issue of seeing who is speeding up, slowing down, when, where, and to what degree. Moves are relative. When evaluating a move's worth, its context, the competition, must be carefully considered. A weak move in a weak field will look better than it is; a strong move in a still stronger field will not, perhaps, look as daunting as it actually was. For example, if a legitimate $35,000 claimer brings his $35,000 speed into play in a field of $20,000 claimers with their $20,000 moves, he might well look like the second coming of Count Fleet. Put that same horse in a feature race, let's say an overnight Handicap, and that selfsame $35,000 move that so impressed against $20,000 horses will leave little to no impression.

You can tell a horse is decelerating when, in relation to the others, he appears to be drifting backward, going, as they say, in the wrong direction. When a horse decelerates in dramatic fashion, he looks like a hapless swimmer being sucked out to sea by a rip tide. The stronger the tide appears to be tugging at him, the more 'used up' the horse. When the process whereby a horse decelerates is especially abrupt, it looks as if the horse in question has either had a heart attack or run into a brick wall.

Conversely, you can tell when a horse brings his speed into play because, in relation to the others, he appears to have suddenly taken wing.

A professional sort 'fires,' brings his speed into play, and it is of little import; chances are he'd best drop down and try cheaper stock.

A horse that mismanages his speed, uses it in a cavalier, inappropriate fashion, and squanders its potential by using it too early or too late will not win many races. With this as context, be wary of horses who expend their speed making middle moves. A horse makes middle moves race after race; it's not a good sign. Lots of 'excuse' horses make middle moves. They look good picking off horses as they go along the backstretch, but come crunch time, when their speed is really needed and the field is driving to the wire, they find themselves empty, their speed nowhere to be found, and with it their ability to do battle. Horses that make middle moves get bet over and over again out of all proportion to their chances of winning. Why? They come with a built-in excuse. "If only he hadn't moved so early", "if only he hadn't moved too late etc." But they don't. Why? It's not in their DNA.

One indication that a horse has a touch of class is when he is used up, clearly out of gas, on empty, running on fumes, so to speak, yet still keeps battling as hard as he can, grudgingly straining not to give an inch. The cheaper the horse, the less quality he has; as soon as he's on empty, he capitulates and folds like a cheap suitcase, no matter how slight the pressure that he encounters.

A horse with quality and then some kicking in and firing, showing his speed, his brilliance, I imagine can be as awesome a sight as a tsunami looming on the horizon. Not that I have ever seen one, or want to. Check out Exceller in the Jockey Gold Cup when he 'fires' and goes up after

Seattle Slew. It's on YouTube. I remember the fellow calling the race getting most excited, his voice rising and trembling with awe as he issued his call, "And it's Exceller; he's got in gear, and he's now flying at the leader." If you're into horse racing, access it; you will get goosebumps.

A powerful move is the equine equivalent of the proverbial irresistible force. The best, most dramatic races occur when an irresistible force comes from off the pace to challenge an immovable object on the lead.

Sometimes when a legitimate horse does not show his speed, it is not because it was absent but rather because he was in against classier stock. If dominated, such a horse may well cease and desist from firing his best shot, his speed. He's been subordinated. He does what he is told. Though locked and loaded, he doesn't pull the trigger. It's a legitimate excuse.

If next time out he 'drops down' and meets the sort that he has shown in the recent past he can boss, he or she has my attention and then some as there are no classier sorts(s) present to intimidate him to the point where his speed will be kept in abeyance.

Besides being familiar with the potency of a horse's best move, his speed, it is beyond important to know when and where it will be brought into play. One cannot hope to accurately foretell the pace of a race, whose chances it will benefit, whose it will hurt, and to what degree if one does not have a handle on when and where all the entrants will 'fire' and bring their speed into play. I cannot stress enough the importance of being eminently conversant with when and where a horse brings his speed into play. It's the key to understanding the pace.

Not having great moves is not the worst thing that can happen to a horse. He can still be a useful professional. If a horse has moves that are simply okay, nothing to write home about, but the intangibles are there and in place, he will be able to win at some level.

I've often wondered how many 'dead pieces' have 'winning ways' and a little bit of class as well but were condemned to abject mediocrity because they lacked the innate athleticism to make a compelling move. If I were such a horse and wanted to win and impose my will, but the ability to kick into a robust enough gear to do so simply wasn't a part of my genetic package, what I'd been gifted with, I'd be bitter, same as if I'd been cursed at birth by a debilitating ailment.

****

All of which brings me yet again to a brief discussion of morning works. Horses can and will show their speed in the morning.

Some horse players are very much into morning workouts. They see them as a key. They study them with the intensity of a Talmudic scholar trying to decipher an especially ambiguous text. I pay little attention to a horse's morning works. I have yet to see anything resembling a correlation between how a horse works and whether or not he wins. Over the years, I have seen far too many 'money burners' sucker folks into throwing away tickets in the afternoon based on moves they made in the morning. If you are a 'rat,' you're a 'rat,' and an impressive morning workout where you flaunt your speed is a moot point. It doesn't change a thing. A 'rat' puts in a sizzling morning work, all it means is that he ran fast when he was all by himself, no pressure, no challenges, no competitions, and winning was not an issue.

On the other hand, day after day, I see real, deal, legitimate, hard-knocking sorts put in tepid, lackluster morning works, but when it is time to play the game and race in the afternoon, they not only run big, they take control and win.

I'm of the considered belief that focusing on morning works is much ado about nothing, sort of like two bald men fighting over a comb. I am always amused when I see people arguing about the significance of a morning work, what they mean, whether it was right for the horse, etc. Ninety nine times out of hundred, the closest any of these folks have ever come to a racehorse is their seat in the grandstand. Yet they question the trainer's competence. Are they so delusional that they actually believe they have a better understanding than the horse's trainer as to the training regimen required for his charge to produce a winning effort? I think not. Just for the record, anyone whose hinge point as to whether or not to make a bet is based on a workout is seriously misguided and will be a donor.

Distance

There is no statute on the books that says the best horse has to win. Other factors come into play and must be considered. If I deem a horse with 'winning ways' to be the class of a field, he garners my attention, and as a serious bet might be in the offing, I commence my due diligence.

I have a checklist. I go through it sort of like a pilot making sure that all systems are in good working order before beginning to taxi for takeoff. Same as a pilot, hopefully, will not take off unless all the boxes on his list have been checked in the affirmative, I will not make a serious bet unless all the boxes on my list have been checked off as well, and all my ducks, so to speak, are in a nice, neat row.

The first box on my list concerns the distance. The distance can be the key. It can easily be the difference between a horse's winning or losing. If I do not believe the distance suits the horse I like, and I cannot in good conscience check off that box I toss the horse out the same as I would a 'dead' piece. If a horse does not pass muster as per all the criteria I use to gauge his chances when doing my due diligence, I pass and look elsewhere for a more suitable opportunity.

When it comes to distance, the vast majority of horses run their best at one, two, or perhaps three distances. For some horses, the distance is irrelevant, as they are able to race and win no matter the distance. Such horses are few and far between; rare orchids indeed. Not many can bring their A game to the table, no matter the distance.

No matter how great the disparity in quality and class between the best horse and the others, I will not invest in the best horse's chances if I believe the distance at hand precludes him from showing his best or that which is quite close to his best form. A horse wins at a distance which is not his strong suit; it's more of a commentary on the woefulness of the field he bested than it is a paean to his prowess and versatility.

The cheaper the horse, the more the distance has to favor him, as do all relevant factors when I'm contemplating wagering on such a horse. In order for me to bet on a cheap yet professional sort, all factors must be in his or her favor and then some, as it doesn't take all that much to throw a cheap horse off his game.

If a professional tries a distance he has never previously attempted, is in good form, competing against the sort of stock he can beat, on a racing surface he likes, and the pace unfolds in his favor, yet he still shows poorly, I have no alternative but to conclude that the distance was the reason for his less than stellar display as it was the only variable in the equation at which he had yet to prove his competence.

People often assume that if a horse likes six and seven furlongs, a mile should be well within his scope. Or that if a horse likes a mile and a 1/16th, he will also like a mile and a 1/8th. Or if a horse likes five furlongs, he will like five ½ furlongs. After all, what's another 1/16th or 1/8th of a mile? The answer, an additional 1/16th of a mile, much less a 1/8th, or a quarter of a mile can be a horse's undoing, the difference between his winning or losing. Assume nothing!

Liking or not liking a distance, like all things that define a thoroughbred, is a trait that can be passed from one generation to the next. A colt or filly whose dam and sire both loved a mile and a quarter is far more likely to like a mile and a quarter than a horse whose dam and sire couldn't stay a step past six furlongs. This does not mean a horse whose parents liked a mile and a quarter is fated to like a mile and a quarter. It just means that the probability of his liking it is far greater than that of a horse whose lineage is composed of horses who could not get a classic distance.

Just for the record, betting on horses to do things based on their breeding is not a good approach. If I had a dollar for every horse that didn't run to his breeding, I'd have long ago purchased my own country, turned it into a monarchy, and installed myself as King.

Unlike table manners, liking a distance cannot be taught. It is what it is, like the color of one's eyes. If a horse is not genetically predisposed to being effective at a particular distance, he cannot be trained to do so. At best, you can train a horse to relax, to use his 'speed' more judiciously, and in so doing, perhaps stretch him out a touch further than his DNA has ordained. But if a horse's stamina is such that a distance is decidedly beyond his scope, it is not going to happen. As my golf pro said to me upon first witnessing my swing, "I can't make chicken salad out of chicken shit."

The key metric I use to determine whether or not a horse likes a distance and has the requisite stamina is the intensity and duration of the speed he can bring into play in a race's later stages. The greater a horse's ability to flex and flaunt his speed in the last 1/16th of a mile, the more I conclude he likes the distance. If a horse is unable to access his speed in the latter stages of a race and has no legitimate excuse to explain its absence, I can only conclude that the distance is not to his liking. A horse cannot accelerate in a meaningful manner in the final stages of a race; it means that at this critical juncture, he cannot effectively challenge for or defend the lead, which does not bode well for his chances of winning.

****

A horse's ability to stay a distance of ground, meaning he can bring his speed into play come crunch time, in the last 1/16th of a mile or so, when push comes to shove and they are driving to the wire, is a function of his stamina. To understand stamina, it is best to think of a horse's speed as being fueled by a canister of high-octane energy labeled SPEED that he carries with him, tucked away, out of sight, in a saddle bag no one can see. This high-octane energy marked SPEED is what fuels his top gear, his speed. Once that canister of SPEED is 'used up' during the course of the race, invested in the quarter mile of a horse's choosing, he can no longer display his speed because the energy needed to do so, his canister of SPEED, has been depleted.

A horse's other energies, not the energy contained in the canister marked SPEED, are what fuel his lesser, cruising gears. A horse lacks the stamina to get a distance, it means that in order for him to simply get to the race's latter stages in somewhat competitive fashion, he has to prematurely tap into and use his SPEED earlier than that which is ideal. This occurs, his 'speed,' his best move, is compromised, as there will be that much less of his SPEED to fuel his all-important endgame, and his chances of winning suffer accordingly. To recap, if the energy, the SPEED, needed to adequately fuel the quarter of mile or so of horse's top gear is diverted to fuel his cruising gears he will then lack the requisite stamina to get the distance at hand as he will not have sufficient speed to bring to the table during the race's denouement which is when and where the issue of who will make their way to the winner's circle is usually decided.

The more stamina a horse has, the more of his SPEED he will have at his fingertips when the wire is looming and the competition is keenest. Two horses 'hook up' at the 1/8th pole. One still has all his SPEED intact; the other horse is on empty, his SPEED having been 'used up' just getting to the 1/8th pole. I know which of the two I want my money on, as I know which of them will accelerate, draw off, and leave the other in his wake.

When they say a horse can stay a distance of ground, what they are really saying is that his SPEED will stay with him and be there for the asking when needed. When they say a horse can 'get' a distance, what they are saying is that his SPEED will get there, whole and intact, and be there when it matters the most.

When all the horses in contention are pretty much 'used up' come the final $1/16^{th}$ of a mile, the race is decided not by which horse is running fastest but rather by which horse is decelerating least rapidly. Betting on a horse because you believe he will be the least 'used up' is betting on a negative. Not a great idea. Figuring out who is the best is tough enough. Figuring out which horse is least worst is far more difficult, as convoluted a conundrum as trying to figure out how many angels can dance on the head of a pin.

A front-runner demonstrates his stamina by showing how long he can stay on the lead at a competitive pace before his SPEED has been used up. If at a mile a frontrunner has already used up all his SPEED just to be on the lead for the first seven furlongs at a competitive pace, come the 1/8th pole, a furlong to go, he will be low-hanging fruit waiting to be plucked.

For horses that close, bring their speed into play from off the pace, the dynamic is somewhat different. Such a horse does not tap into his SPEED during a race's early stages. Rather, they hope to carry it intact, as an Air Force bomber would its ordinance, and then deploy it when it matters most, in the drive to the wire.

If a closer lacks the stamina to stay a particular distance, same as a front-runner who can't, it means he must tap into his SPEED earlier than he would want, thus depleting it and lessening its impact when and if it is finally brought into play.

A 'used up' frontrunner can win if the horses closing on him are also 'used up' and decelerating at a more rapid pace than he is. If this is not the case and the horses closing in on him are moving at a faster pace than he is, the frontrunner will only win if those closing in on him run out of ground and he is able to reach the sanctuary of the wire before they overtake him.

The only way a 'used up' closer can win is if the horses in front of him that he is trying to run down are 'used up' worse than he is and decelerating and drifting backward at a more rapid rate.

Because of the manner in which closers run, they often give the illusion that the wire arrived too soon. That if they just had a little more distance, they would have surely won. A closer 'fires,' makes a huge closing run at six furlongs, and just comes up short; it is easy and somewhat intuitive to conclude that had the race been a touch longer, he would have prevailed. That would be a mistake. Just because a closer can 'fire' at six furlongs does not mean he has the stamina to bring his 'speed' into play and 'fire' at a longer distance. I have seen many a closer run awesomely through the stretch at six furlongs but, when asked to go further, come up empty. Why? They lack the requisite stamina and must tap into their SPEED earlier than that which is optimal. Stretching a closer out who came up short at a lesser distance may be the answer, and then again, it may not.

If a professional sort loses because of the distance, it is a legitimate excuse.

A horse does not have to win at a distance in order for me to conclude it suits him. It's about his speed and how much of it he can bring to the party late. To illustrate, a horse has 'winning ways' and has shown he can win at six furlongs. His connections decide to test him, get a handle on whether or not he can stay two turns at a mile and 1/16th. It's a nine-horse field. Five are 'dead pieces,' and four are legitimate horses I respect. Three of the four legitimate horses, save the horse trying the distance for the first time, have all shown they can win at a mile and 1/16th. The sprinter attempting the distance for the first time is a front runner. He wants to set the pace, be on the lead, and control it throughout, as is a front runner's wont. One of the other 'live pieces' is a front-runner as well. He, too, wants the lead. Another 'live piece' is a stalker, meaning he'll sit right behind the pace setters. The other professional is a mid-pack closer. He'll sit four or five lengths back of the stalker and will 'fire,' and bring his speed into play midway around the turn, and commence his challenge from there.

They break. The two front runners 'hook up.' They round the first turn. Both the stalkers and the mid-pack closer assume their respective positions as they make their way around the clubhouse turn, and move along the backstretch. The two front runners, one of whom is trying the distance for the first time, 'hook up.' Neither gives an inch. They set a blistering pace. At the half-mile pole, the colt trying the distance for the first time puts the other away, takes control, and continues on. Clearly, he has been hard-used. At the 5/16th pole, the stalker makes his move. He 'hooks' the leader as they straighten for home. The first-timer digs in and battles back. They go head-to-head. Another furious battle. The first-timer puts the grudgingly game stalker away at the 1/16th pole. Even to an unpracticed eye, the leader now appears weary, shortening stride and decelerating from his efforts. At this point, the mid-pack closer commences his run, reaches the leader, and engages him 70 yards from the wire. Though clearly spent, the first-timer digs in and tries to keep his latest challenger at bay. The horse trying the distance for the first time is running on fumes. Though his heart is willing, his flesh is out of gas and thirty yards from the wire, he is headed and surrenders. He's had enough. He loses. He comes in third by four lengths. A late plodder runs past him and grabs second. Though he lost, clearly he can stay a mile and 1/16th. He has, to say the least, a legitimate excuse, the pace at which he was forced to run throughout. He never got a breather. Those that ascribe the key to his losing as being a function of the distance and not the pace will not only miss out on an opportunity to cash a ticker next time he tries that distance, but even worse, they might lose money betting against him.

On the other hand, if the colt trying the mile and 1/16th for the first time was the only speed, got to set a soft, self-serving pace, went unchallenged throughout, and then came up empty in the stretch, went backward, and was inhaled by a wall of horses coming from behind, I would know with an uncommon certainty that he is unable to stay a mile and a 1/16th. Going forward, I would not bet him at a mile and 1/16th with Monopoly money. Not only do the races speak to me, but I like to think I listen.

The distances a horse likes are usually contiguous. I see a horse win at a mile, and mile and 1/8, I'll bet him to win the first time he tries a mile and 1/16th, or a mile and 70 yards. In the same vein, if a horse likes seven furlongs, a mile and a 1/16th, and a mile and a quarter, I would have no compunction whatsoever betting on him to win at a mile and 70 yards or a mile and 1/8th.

The one exception to my contiguity rule is seven furlongs. In my experience, seven furlongs is a most problematic distance. When it comes to seven furlongs, I take nothing for granted. If I see a horse win at six furlongs and then at a mile or beyond, I will not automatically conclude that he will like seven furlongs. I've seen horses that loved six furlongs, loved a mile, and were useless at seven furlongs.

Seven furlongs is a most enigmatic distance, and not many horses perform to their optimum at seven furlongs. If I come across a horse that is a seven-furlong specialist, I treasure him, as they are few and far between. As to why seven furlongs have such strange properties, I have no idea. Seven furlongs, or so it seems, for me, is the Bermuda Triangle of racing.

Stamina is highly valued. We embrace it and respect thoroughbreds that can stay a classic distance of ground, a mile and a quarter or a mile and a half, in the same way, we applaud and revere things that stand the test of time as opposed to a flash in the pan. Think Cole Porter as opposed to a one-hit-wonder. The sort of stamina that a horse has to have in order to stay a classic distance is one of the many ideals a thoroughbred is bred to express. If two horses are of the same class, imbued with similar talent, but one can stay a classic distance of ground, and the other cannot, the former is more highly valued, with the differential in their respective worth reflected in their stud fees. Please note that just because a horse can stay a classic distance of a mile and a quarter does not mean he can stay a classic distance of a mile and a half. History is littered with those who failed to secure the Triple Crown because they were incapable of staying the Belmont's mile-and-half distance, a race aptly referred to as the 'test of Champions.'

For reasons that escape me, nowadays the Belmont Stakes is the only race that tests a horse on the dirt in a Grade I event at a mile and a half. I don't get it. A mile and a half tests and plumbs the depths of a horse's quality as no other. I guess it simply doesn't sit well in a world that has grown habituated to sound bites and instant gratification. Apparently, mile-and-half tests, like the art of good conversation, appear to be one of the things we've jettisoned and left behind like so much excess baggage as we rush off to nowhere just for the sake of going there.

The great drama surrounding the Kentucky Derby resides in the fact that it is the first time promising young horses with classic bloodlines are tested by a classic distance, the Derby's mile and a quarter. None of the Derby's three-year-old entrants have yet to race beyond a mile and 1/8th. First Saturday in May, come nightfall, lots of breeders and owners dreams of breeding and/or owning a classic horse will lie in ruins as the Derby can and will expose a colt's inability to stay a classic distance of ground.

Surfaces

If I conclude the best horse can handle the distance, I move on to the next item on my list, the racing surface. If I'm of the opinion that the horse I think best does not care for the racing surface he is slated to race on, I will not make a serious bet. Perhaps it is not all that sporting of me, but I have to believe all relevant factors are in my favor before I make a serious bet. I try, as best, I can, to leave as little as possible to the vagaries of chance.

My senior year in college, I was randomly selected to take a test as part of an experiment sponsored by the Psychology department. I was paid 10 dollars. The test took about an hour. The following week, I was informed that my test indicated that I liked to win arguments. I asked them to elaborate. They wouldn't. I think that they wanted me to argue with them because, in doing so, I would then be giving credence to their thesis, and that I did indeed like to argue. Looking back, now in retrospect, what I think the test tells me is that when my horse wins, I find it most satisfying because it's as if I'd won an argument with all the bettors who bet against the horse I deemed best.

I also find winning a most pleasing experience because the act of my being correct, the validation involved, causes my body, for reasons unknown, to celebrate by producing and releasing substances into my bloodstream that affect me in the same manner I imagine certain controlled substances would. After a win, especially if it's a serious bet, one in which that much more of my ego was invested, a feeling of muted ebullience envelopes me, and I carry myself for a while with a subtle yet decided swagger.

When I win, perhaps my body releases dopamine, the drug that causes one to experience a 'runner's high.' I have no means of comparison. Granted, earlier on I strongly noted that there is no such thing as a stone-cold certainty. I will now qualify that statement. It is a stone-cold certainty that the longest stretch of ground that I will ever run, certainly not long enough to trigger a runner's high, is from my couch to the refrigerator and back again in order to snatch a cold beer during a commercial.

$$\text{*************************}$$

As a racing surface can bring out both the best and worst in a horse, I place great importance on knowing whether or not a horse likes the surface he is being asked to race on. The class of the field likes the surface he's going to race on, I like his chances that much more. If he doesn't, my due diligence as to his chances comes to an abrupt halt, and I throw him out the same as I would if he were being asked to run at a distance that wasn't within his scope.

Dirt racing surfaces are composed of differing recipes of clay, gravel, soil, synthetics, chemicals, and God knows what else. No two dirt surfaces are exactly alike. All, to one degree or another, play differently. Even if they were constructed exactly alike in both material and proportion, the ambient atmospherics, the climate they dwell in, would cause them to ripen differently. Lay the same exact surface at Turf Paradise, Gulfstream, and Aqueduct, and eventually, over time, they will manifest different properties. Turf Paradise, Arizona, is hot and arid; Gulfstream, Miami, suffers from heat, humidity, and rain; while Aqueduct, located on the South Eastern edge of Queens, abutting the Brooklyn border, is constantly freezing and thawing, snowed on, and is often set upon by fierce, cold, moisture-laden winds that come howling in off nearby Jamaica Bay. Go to Aqueduct in the winter months, I suggest you dress warmly.

In addition, further exacerbating their differences, racing surfaces are also ministered to differently as per the beliefs and methods employed by the track superintendent, whose approach to maintaining the surface they are responsible for can differ, same as golf course superintendents can differ in regards to how thick and high they believe the rough should be, the width of the fairways, the speed of the greens, etc.

There are horses for which the surface is irrelevant. They perform at their best, whatever that might be, no matter the surface: dirt, grass, and any permutation thereof. Such horses, though, are few and far between.

A horse doesn't like a surface; it is a legitimate excuse.

In my experience, the better the horse is, the more likely it is that the footing will not be an issue. The cheaper the horse, the more of a difference it can make, as the cheaper a horse is, the less wiggle room there is when it comes to his dealing with hardship. A horse doesn't like a racing surface; it is a form of adversity. The cheaper the horse, the easier it is for him to use the surface as an excuse to pack it in and not put forth his best effort. Which is why it is possible to claim such a horse for the price of a 15-year-old car that is in need of both a new exhaust system and a set of both brakes and tires.

A surface's impact on a horse's performance can be dramatic. I've seen horses who were able to win Grade I events on one surface morph into 'dead pieces' on another.

With one slight difference, I use the same litmus test to determine if a horse likes a surface that I use to determine if he likes a particular distance, and that is his ability to show his 'speed.' In order to show he likes a distance, a horse has to be able to bring his 'speed' into play in the last $1/16^{th}$ of the event. In order for a horse to show me he likes a surface, that he can run on it effectively, all he has to do is show me his 'speed,' only I don't care at what point in the race he brings it into play. If he is able to show his 'speed,' it means he is okay with the surface. If he is not able to show his 'speed,' if the footing precludes him from doing so, his winning becomes that much more problematic, and I will not invest in his chances. The more 'speed' that a horse is able to flash, no matter when and where he does so during the course of a race, the more I know the surface is conducive to his showing his best.

A horse shows his speed yet loses, I know the surface wasn't the issue no matter how far back he finishes; that the key to his poor performance lies elsewhere, i.e., distance, pace, class, whatever. If next time out, on the same surface, and the factor that my post-race analysis told me was the key to his disquieting previous performance is no longer in play, I'll have no qualms betting him.

When a surface precludes a horse from showing his 'speed,' it can appear to the observer that the horse is laboring somewhat, as if he is unable to dig in, grab hold, and gain purchase, causing him to lack the requisite leverage needed to accelerate; sort of like a car with a compromised clutch that is unable to change gears.

Liking or not liking a particular racing surface is a trait, like class, stamina, and 'winning ways,' that I believe can be passed from one generation to the next. A colt or filly whose dam and sire loved the turf is far more likely to like the turf than the offspring of a sire and dam that loathed the grass. Still, it's just a matter of potential and percentages. Betting on a horse to like a footing because his lineage suggests he will like it is a bad idea, as it contravenes my mandate never to bet on a horse to do something until he has done it.

That being said, there was a situation where an exception was made, and I bet horses the first time they tried the grass based solely on their bloodlines. By the time his second or third crop came to the races, it was apparent that the offspring of Stage Door Johnny loved the turf, took to it like ducks to water, and upon encountering the turf for the first time, moved up several notches and behaved like real racehorses. No matter how abysmally a Stage Door Johnny performed on the dirt, the first time his hooves stepped on the grass, he was transformed, as if sprinkled with pixie dust, into a horse to be reckoned with. I like to think that I accept and accommodate reality rather than dig in my heels and deny it, so I proposed to the Executive Rules Committee (ERC) of which I'm Chairman, that betting on Stage Door Johnny's first time they took to the turf should no longer be proscribed and, in fact, encouraged. After a bit of debate, some of it heated, there was a roll call, a vote was taken, and then just like that, it was official: betting on colts and fillies sired by Stage Door Johnny the first time they tried the grass was allowed. The Executive Racing Committee (ERC), me, applauded my decision. No other offspring have ever been given similar leeway. As a matter of fact, once or twice similar situations were brought to the ERC's attention, but the issue was tabled and never even brought to a vote. Stage Door Johnny's offspring were unique.

If a legitimate kind of horse who has checked all the other boxes on my punch list, save for the racing surface, upon trying a surface for the first time shows nothing and runs evenly throughout, never flashing any sort of a move, much less his 'speed,' I assume the surface was indeed at fault, as it was the lone variable that had yet to be accounted for. Next time out, if the same horse runs in similar circumstances on a surface I know he likes, and he's able to bring his 'speed' into play, I am then pretty much well convinced that the key to his desultory performance in his previous race was the footing.

Betting on a horse to do something he hasn't done and then losing is like shooting yourself in the foot.

When a particular venue brings out the very best in a horse, he is said to be 'a horse for a course.' It's as if the venue is the horse's Fairy Godmother and she casts a spell on his behalf that makes him as good as he can be. Knowing when a horse is a 'horse for a course' is a good thing to know.

Whenever I think of a horse for a course, I think of General Assembly at Saratoga. If the Triple Crown races had all been run at Saratoga, he most certainly would have worn the Crown. When General Assembly raced at Saratoga, it was as if he had imbibed a secret elixir that endowed him with an uncommon awesomeness. He raced four times at Saratoga, and the competition still hasn't come close to sniffing him. At two, he romped in the Saratoga Special and then decimated the field in the Grade I Hopeful. At three, he lorded it over the field in a seven-furlong prep for the Travers, and then in the Travers toyed with a field that wasn't half bad in what can only be described as a romp. If memory serves me correctly, he set the track record that day for a mile and a quarter. General Assembly was good, really good, and acquitted himself with glory at any and all venues where he competed. But at Saratoga, I'm telling you, he took it to another level and was about as good as a racehorse can be.

Liking or not liking a race course is an aspect of a horse's form that does not change. In my experience, if a horse has an aptitude for a course, he will show well at that venue throughout his career, provided, of course, he is in good form.

Sometimes it takes a horse a race or two before he gets comfortable with a new surface, gets the hang of it, so to speak, but once he does gain that liking, he will always like it, and it will no longer be an impediment to my investing in his chances.

Liking a surface is just one factor in a very complex matrix. No matter how much a horse likes a particular course, if he is spotted inappropriately, in poor form, or the pace hurts his chances, or he loathes the distance, etc., he will not show well.

Sometimes a horse that has been a bit of a ne'er-do-well, an abject loser, suddenly, for no apparent reason, displays 'winning ways' when shipped to a new venue, and then, as if his brain has been rebooted, his newfound approach becomes a permanent part of his repertoire, and he commences to evidence the intangibles wherever he races. If this occurs, I must reconfigure my opinion. Nothing is set in stone, and if you are not moving forward, you're going backward.

And then sometimes, sadly, upon shipping out from the venue where a horse has discovered and unlocked the potential intangibles that dwelt within him, he backslides and returns to being dismal.

A horse loves a track; sometimes I wonder if it is not just the surface that he has taken to, but that he finds the ambiance at the venue, its total gestalt, most salubrious, and that is what puts him in fine fettle and brings out the best in him. Maybe it's a combination of the sights, the sounds, the smells, the way the breezes stir the treetops, the morning birdsong, the smell of lilacs wafting through the barn, the water? Who knows?

If a professional who has raced horribly at a venue which he hates returns to a surface I know he likes, I pay careful attention. An amenable surface might be just what the Doctor ordered to return him to relevance and provide a breath of fresh air that will blow him free of the racing doldrums in which he has been becalmed. He runs well; he's back on my radar, as I know his recent woefulness was a function of the venue he was at.

I won't, however, bet on him the first time back based solely on what he once was. Current form matters.

One of the few times I take note of a horse's workouts is when a horse that is on my radar tries a track he has never run on. If he puts in morning work where he flashes his speed, I then know he likes the surface, and if he does lose in the afternoon, I will know it was not because of the footing. That the key to his losing lies elsewhere.

A horse on my radar shows pedestrian works at the new track I take a wait-and-see approach till he actually competes before I come to a decision one way or the other as to his aptitude for the footing. The reason he didn't show his speed in the morning might be for the simple reason that his trainer saw no need to do so.

An eye-popping, bullet-type work in the morning counts for nothing if the horse laying it down is a 'morning glory.' 'Morning glories' don't have a clue. They are moot points. They lack the intangibles. Same goes for money burners like 'rats', 'dogs', horses with 'seconditis', etc.

I have no compunction betting on a real, deal, hard-knocking sort the first time he competes at a track where he has never raced if such a horse has shown his quality and 'speed' at any number of tracks. A horse has run well, shown his 'speed' at Laurel, Delaware, Gulfstream, and the Fair Grounds, then ships into, let's say, Tampa Bay, I might well bet him his first time out. My assumption is that he's performed like a legitimate sort everywhere else he's run; why should Tampa Bay be different? Sometimes it is different, the one track he doesn't care for, and I lose. But over the long haul, when all is said and done, I've done well with this approach.

If a horse is stabled at a racetrack where he loathes the footing, he is not going to have much of a career. If I owned a cheap horse that couldn't get out of his own way at the track where my stable was headquartered, and nothing my trainer did improved the situation, I'd ship him elsewhere. Maybe that's the answer. I know, it's grasping at straws, but what the heck, I'd give it a try. Perhaps, just perhaps, a different surface is the secret sauce that will turn him into a real racehorse. It may or may not be the answer, but it's certainly worth asking the question.

All of which makes me wonder how many horses have had lackluster careers for the simple reason that the fates conspired in such a fashion that they languished at tracks where the surfaces were antithetical to their showing well, while out there, somewhere, someplace, there were track(s) where they might have been a 'horse for a course' and flourished.

Not only does one have to take account of a particular surface, but one must also consider all its various permutations: fast, wet fast, good slow, muddy, or sloppy. Just because a horse likes a surface does not mean he will care for any and all of the identities it might assume.

I do not make serious bets on tracks labeled otherwise: sloppy, muddy, slow, etc. It's a race track cliché that finding winners on off-tracks is like stealing candy from a baby. Simply find a horse with the highest turn of early foot who likes an off-track and watch him go wire to wire. As a rule of thumb, horses who gain the early lead become that much harder to catch and overtake in the slop, as sloppy tracks are the least tiring of surfaces, and as such, allow a horse with early speed to stretch his SPEED far more than he could on a track labeled Fast, Wet Fast, or Good. And because the surface is less tiring when such a frontrunner is 'used up,' when and if he slips into deceleration mode, he will decelerate far less dramatically than when he is used up on a Fast, Good, or Slow track. Which makes it that much more difficult for a horse coming from off the pace to make up the ground separating him from the leader, much less engaging, 'hooking' and putting that leader away.

I don't bet races on off-tracks for the simple reason that, over the years, I have witnessed on such tracks no shortage of bizarre, inexplicable, and inscrutable results, none of which were in my best interests. I've seen too many off-tracks where moribund 'dead pieces' ran as if they were a reincarnated, updated, supercharged version of Whirlaway. I've been burned so many times in the slop that nowadays, on such days, I stay home.

As for those who assert that locating a winner on an off-track is as easy as breaking twigs, all I have to say in rebuttal is, "except when it isn't." Remember, there is no such thing as a free lunch.

I also eschew betting on races run on off-tracks because of the paltry payouts one can expect to receive from tabbing such a winner. Even the dimmest of bettors, those with the racetrack sophistication of a not particularly bright sixth grader, know that off-tracks favor the early speed. Such a horse wins, he or she will invariably be a big-time underlay as everyone and his mother will have bet on the horse.

Some horses can handle both the turf and the dirt. Others cannot. Never, and I mean never, conclude that just because a horse can handle one, he will be as adept at the other. I've seen Grade I Stakes winners on the dirt who couldn't run a lick on the grass, and vice versa.

Save for the offspring of Stage Door Johnny I have never bet on a horse to 'grass' until he has shown me he can. I've been waiting for the next Stage Door Johnny to appear, same as some await the coming of the Messiah.

I use the same metric to determine if a horse likes the grass as I do to determine if he likes a dirt surface, and that is, whether or not and to what degree he is able to express his best move, his 'speed.'

Unlike a dirt surface, I don't have to see a horse compete over a particular grass course before I invest in his chances. Grass is grass. A horse likes competing on the grass. I find that it doesn't matter all that much where the grass is growing.

If a legitimate sort of horse has run creditably on the dirt at Gulfstream ships into Monmouth, I won't bet him at Monmouth until I see how and to what degree he is able to express his speed on Monmouth's dirt track. However, under the same circumstances, a horse has shown he can handle the turf at Gulfstream and ships into Monmouth to compete on the grass; I assume he'll like it. My belief, a horse can run on the turf; he can run on the turf no matter where it is sown, grown, watered, and manicured. Until this hypothesis begins dispensing negative outcomes, I will run with it, no pun intended.

Same as I only bet on dirt tracks that are Fast, Wet Fast, or Good, I only bet on grass surfaces that are labeled Firm, Good, or Hard. I pay no attention to races run on Soft or Yielding turf. I do so for the same reason I avoid betting on muddy or sloppy tracks. I've seen too many bizarre, surreal results unfold on such turf.

Of late, certain venues are replacing their dirt tracks with synthetic, all-weather surfaces. The idea of horses racing on plastic derivatives rubs me the wrong way. It appears to be an egregious affront to the natural order of things. Yet another step in the wrong direction.

There are different types of all-weather tracks. Just because a horse shows his 'speed' on one does not mean he will transfer that skill set to another. Again, the litmus test for an all-weather surface, as it is for any surface is: can a horse bring his 'speed' into play, and if so, to what degree?

Then there is the rarest of the rare, a horse that can compete at the highest level no matter the surface or distance. Kelso comes to mind. No horse has ever compiled a more noteworthy career. Five years in a row he was voted Horse of the Year, and during his tenure, every Fall the best of the current crop of three-year-old colts would come calling in the hope of taking Kelso's measure, and always they, not Kelso, were found wanting. Kelso could win against top-flight competition at any distance, from six furlongs to two miles, on any kind of surface on either dirt or grass. He was beyond special. When Kelso passed, fabled racing columnist Joe Hirsch, wordsmith that he was, brilliantly commenced the column in which he eulogized the great gelding when he wrote, "Once upon a time there was a horse named Kelso, but only once."

Pace

If the horse I think best passes muster as per the distance and the racing surface, I move on to the next item on my checklist, the pace. My goal, understand how the pace will impact the amount of SPEED, relative to the competition, the horse who, in my opinion, is best, will have at his disposal in the last 70 or so yards, when races, for the most part, are won or lost.

I do not deconstruct the pace in the hope that my analysis will elucidate a winner. I've already selected the horse I think best. I parse the pace solely to see if it validates his or her chances.

If I conclude, the pace will hurt the chances of the horse I think best, I am then left with the somewhat daunting task of determining whether or not the disparity in quality between the horse I think best and the others is so great, of such magnitude, that the rigors the pace will impose will preclude his winning. Unless the answer to this query is an egregious no it will not, I keep my hands in my pockets.

I believe it is worth noting, as I believe it to be a foundational notion: never, ever bet against the horse you think best, as such a decision can come back to haunt you. Even if I think the pace will devastate the best horse's chances and profoundly elevate the chances of another by several or so notches and then some, I will not bet against the best horse. Betting against the best horse is the racetrack equivalent of pissing into the wind.

One day, a long-standing friend of mine, Phil, bet against the horse he thought best, a favorite of his no less, because he thought the pace was going to be so antithetical to the horse's chances that he couldn't possibly win. Apparently the horse Phil bet against, the horse he thought best, apparently got wind of the fact that Phil was betting against him, took it as a personal insult and as if to both make and prove a point, won for fun, eased up, under wraps. Phil lost it. He exploded. Ranted and raved like a lunatic. He was so annoyed at himself, so irked, so flummoxed, that he didn't look where he was going, fell down a flight of steps, and broke his leg. Only time in my life I've seen a compound fracture. It wasn't pretty. He was on crutches for months.

Fat Larry the Lip, another acquaintance, made a strange gurgling sound and then fainted upon spying a jagged piece of Pete's tibia poking out of Pete's shin like a hitchhiker's thumb pleading for a ride. Upon fainting, Fat Larry the Lip hit his head on the arm of a seat and knocked out three of his front teeth. All in all, it was a memorable day.

Fat Larry was known as the Lip because he talked a lot. It also served to distinguish him from another hefty Larry who hung out with us who was known by the moniker Bald Larry. I always wondered, statistically, what are the chances that of the ten or so guys who you regularly hang out with at the track, two will be named Larry and both will be borderline obese.

By the time Bald Larry was 25, he didn't have a hair on his head. He had a few hairs curling out of his nose and ears, but nothing growing atop his head, which was as barren as the surface of the moon. He always wore a hat, a fedora. Bald Fat Larry was a bit of a loudmouth and a know-it-all, and when he was not in earshot, he was referred to one by and all as the Fat Fuck.

A professional sort loses due to an inimical pace; it is a legitimate excuse.

I pay close attention to the pace. The two best horses I ever saw were Doctor Fager and Seattle Slew. I saw both lose because the pace they encountered one particular afternoon was so antithetical to their chances, so toxic, they were unable to overcome the adversity it imposed. If the pace can cause Dr. Fager and Seattle Slew to lose, imagine the havoc it can play with the chances of a cheap claimer.

Picking a winner entails a lot of figuring. Of all the things one has to figure, the pace is the toughest, the easiest to get wrong. Figuring pace is nuanced, a considerably sized can of worms that once opened, can cause all sorts of head-scratching issues to emerge. And oftentimes, it seems that each new issue begets additional new issues, each of which in turn spawns yet more issues, and so on and so forth until one is overwhelmed. Figuring pace is a far more complex undertaking than figuring which horse is dominant, if a horse has 'winning ways,' and whether or not a horse likes or dislikes a distance, or a racing surface. The pace involves lots of moving parts. Figuring out how it will unfold is a convoluted process littered with ambiguity. Gray areas abound. Figuring pace is anything but cut and dried. It is not a day at the beach. If, at the end of my figuring, I find the arguments that justify my prognostications as to how the pace will unfold to be especially intricate and convoluted, I know I have most probably figured wrong.

Some are of the opinion that 'pace is the name of the game,' that it's the penultimate key. In my opinion, it is just another piece of the puzzle, albeit an important one. Though I do not believe it is as important a factor in determining who wins as the depth and intensity of a horse's intangibles, the pace can easily be the key.

The fundamental principle from which the impact of the pace is deduced, whose chances it will benefit, whose it will hurt, and to what degree, is as follows: the slower the early pace, the better it is for a horse that uses his SPEED early; the faster the early pace, the more advantageous it is for a horse that uses his SPEED late to close on the leader(s) and run them down from behind. The devil, of course, is in the details. All other notions regarding pace are derivative. I'm reminded of what Maimonides said when queried by the Moors as to the Old Testaments message. Maimonides responded, "Do unto others as you would have others do unto you. All else is commentary."

When the pace unfolds exactly as I envisioned it, or pretty close to it, I feel empowered, somewhat sublime, as clearly, I was able to see the future while it still stalked out of sight beyond the horizon, no more palpable than a daydream.

Such feelings, though, are highly perishable. Trust me, they can vanish after the next race and leave me wondering how I could possibly be so dense. If the races do one thing, they ensure that you never get too big for your britches. Soon as you figure you have a grip on things, what's it all about, you find out you don't. At the races, it is easy to overreach and fall flat on your face, like Icarus when he had the temerity to reach for the heavens and flew too close to the sun, whereupon his wings melted, he plummeted back to earth, and face planted.

My philosophy at the track, especially when contemplating the pace and its impact, is congruent with 'Occam's Razor'; that is, the correct answer is usually the one that requires the fewest assumptions. An assumption is a leap of faith, a subset of wishing and hoping. That's what makes the pace so tricky. Figuring the pace can generate assumptions, scads of them; as it is as fecund an environment for generating assumptions as a rabbit hutch is for producing floppy-eared little bunnies.

The pace of a race is the rate at which it unfolds. Where and when it speeds up, slows down, and to what degree. Acceleration and deceleration are its yin and yang. The pace is determined by when and where horses bring their SPEED into play.

For the purpose of figuring the pace, I categorize runners into six basic types based on how they use their SPEED. They are: front runners that do not rate; front runners that do; stalkers; horses who close from mid-pack; horses that close from way back; and horses that close from so far back that they appear to be running in a different zip code. This categorization of running styles is just a broad rule of thumb, a heuristic schemata that I use as a starting point from which to delve into the myriad subtleties as to how the pace of a race might unfold.

Front runners use their speed to throw down as soon as they break the gate. A thoroughbred who can bring his

SPEED into play from the onset is said to have 'early foot'. First jump, such frontrunners compete with similar-minded front runners to determine which of them will stamp their will upon the other, gain control of the lead, and with it, the right to set the pace, and in so doing, display their dominance. A front runner's competitive juices are such that he wishes to lead, and be in front from start to finish. In a nutshell, his strategy is, "I'm in front; catch me, 'hook' me, and put me away if, of course, you have the wherewithal to do so."

Front runners are able to reach their top speed, or close to it, from a standing start. They are like cars that can go from zero to 60 in a matter of seconds. A horse with 'early foot' does not have to shift from first to second to third in order to engage his penultimate gear. A horse has a front-runner's mindset, the desire and need to lead throughout, but lacks the sort of 'early foot' required to compete in such fashion he is a moot point that will soon be culled.

It is to the front-runner's benefit that he dominates and puts away the other early speed, if there is any, and takes control of the lead as quickly as possible. The quicker he is able to vanquish similarly minded runners, if indeed there are any, the less arduous the process, the less of his SPEED will be used to accomplish that end. Thus, he will have that much more of his SPEED to deploy when and if he is engaged by a closer(s) who takes a run and comes calling in the hope of taking control of the lead later on in the proceedings.

I perceive two types of front runners. A frontrunner who cannot 'rate' uses his trump card, his speed, as soon as the gate flies open and then continues to play that card over and over again till his SPEED is depleted, whereupon he commences to decelerate. Such a runner's Achilles Heel resides in the fact that even after garnering the early lead and having put the competition away, he will continue to use his SPEED to go as fast as he can for as long as he can. It doesn't matter to him if he is 'hooked up,' battling for supremacy, or 10 lengths clear of the field; he still goes as fast as he can, of his own volition, needlessly using himself up.

Therefore, when and if a closer(s) comes calling for the lead, he will have that much less of his SPEED with which to do battle and defend the lead.

A front-runner who does not rate treats his SPEED as if it is inexhaustible, a bubbling spring that will never run dry. He compromises his chances for no good reason. In terms of racing efficiency, his mindset is flawed. He's profligate and wasteful. He's his own worst enemy. Rather than making things easier on himself, he makes things harder. It is as if he is intent on stacking the deck against himself. If SPEED were money, it would quickly burn a hole in his pocket.

This is not to say such front-runners never win. The only time they do so is if the horses racing behind them are of the woeful variety and none of them are able to mount much of a closing move, much less a significant one because if they were able to do so, they would most assuredly gain the lead as the 'used up' frontrunner, now devoid of his SPEED and with it, his ability to accelerate and do battle is low-hanging fruit ripe for the taking.

The only time I consider betting such a frontrunner is if he has 'winning ways,' even though he goes about doing so in a somewhat half-assed manner, and he is the class of the field and then some, much the best, meaning no horse who closes on and 'hooks' him will be able to get past him no matter how weary he might be because he is, relatively speaking, an overwhelmingly dominant presence.

A front-runner that can and will rate is able to dole out his SPEED, husband it, keep it in abeyance, and save it for when and where it is most needed. Frontrunners that can rate do not piss away their SPEED for no good reason. I'm a big fan of such horses. I have confidence in them. I appreciate and respect the manner in which they go about their business. They make for good wagers.

The modus operandi for such a frontrunner is that he vies to control the lead as early on as possible, the same as a frontrunner who will not rate. However, once he has bossed the others and taken control of the early lead, and his SPEED is no longer needed; he throttles back and downshifts to a lesser, more energy-efficient gear. In doing so, he saves whatever of his SPEED he has left, so it will be there for the asking should it be needed later, if and when a closer(s) comes calling. A closer launches a challenge against such a front-runner after said front-runner has established his hegemony over the field, said front-runner, having saved what was left of his SPEED for just such an occasion, will step on the gas, tap into what remains of his SPEED, accelerate, and do battle with the erstwhile usurper, and hopefully he will still have enough left in the tank to dispense with the challenger. If our frontrunner puts away said closer he again downshifts, and throttles back. Yet again saving whatever remnants of his SPEED he still has left in case yet another closer comes calling.

Front runners who rate use their SPEED most constructively. They treat their SPEED as the precious resource it is and use it only when and if their control of the lead is threatened. They use their SPEED thoughtfully, strategically, in a manner that best enhances their chances of winning. Such horses are miserly with their SPEED. They spend it wisely. When it comes to their SPEED, they are most prudent. They're like people who put something away for a rainy day.

When the best horse is a front-runner that can rate, he gets my full attention and then some. If he is the only speed in the race, will acquire the lead for a song, and steal away from the others like a thief in the night, employing his lesser gears and using little to any of his SPEED, I think of Voltaire when he looked around, assessed the situation, and concluded, 'This is the best of all possible worlds.' When I come across such a situation, I'm elated and amazed at my good fortune, the same as if I were an avid bird watcher who had stumbled upon and been able to positively identify an esoteric, rarely seen species.

The only thing that can dissuade me from buying a ticket when the best horse is a frontrunner that rates is if the field is laden with quality horses. I'm especially wary if a goodly number of those with quality are front runners as well. Their presence and the struggles that may ensue to take control of the early lead may well be of the withering, scorching variety that will suck the life out of all those involved, including the front-runner I think best. Afterward, if indeed the competition was as good as I thought to be, after putting the other front runners away, the horse I think best may well be a shadow of the horse he was when he broke the gate as is SPEED may have been used up to such a degree that what he has left to do battle with doesn't amount to a hill of beans. A frontrunner, no matter how dominant, has just so much SPEED, and can fight just so many battles. A horse wins the early lead, the race within the race, no matter how good he might be, it may well be a Pyrrhic victory.

If the best horse, a frontrunner that can rate is the only speed in the race, he is said to sit the 'garden trip.' A horse sits the 'garden trip,' it means that he is ideally positioned to take maximum advantage of whatever benefits the pace might provide.

****

I'm of the opinion that horses that 'fire' and come from behind are inherently disadvantaged by their approach. A frontrunner can, at times, shape the pace to his advantage by slowing it down once he has secured the lead and it is safely in his grasp. A closer has no such recourse. He has no choice but to deal with the pace that is carved out in front of him. The cards he plays are not of his choosing. If the pace up front is slow, aiding and abetting the chances of a horse on the lead, a closer can do nothing to subvert the situation and ease his burden, the adversity that is being heaped upon him.

Another bit of adversity that a horse who comes from off the pace may encounter, that is rarely an issue for a horse running forwardly, is that he is far more likely to encounter traffic problems. Like getting squeezed back, forced wide, blocked, bumped, impeded, clipping heels, etc.

A closer might also have to deal with dirt being kicked back in his face from those he is in arrears of. I imagine that dealing with clods of dirt being hurled back into a horse's face like a barrage of anti-aircraft flak can at times be a distinctly disquieting experience that might well cool a horse's competitive ardor. This is an issue, and a vexatious one at that, that horses racing forwardly do not have to deal with.

Yet another issue to be considered when parsing the chances of a closer is that if and when the closer does close and commences his run at the leader, the simple act of his making up the ground that separates him from the horse(s) he is going up after, forces him to accelerate and, in so doing, tap into his SPEED. The further back he 'fires' from, the more of his SPEED he will have to use to simply make up the ground that separates him from the horse(s) in front of him he is attempting to reach, much less that which is required for him to successfully engage the leader(s). Ironically, in such a situation, especially if the pace has been somewhat languid when a closer does reach and engage the horse(s) he is in pursuit of, it is the closer whose SPEED may well be more depleted than the SPEED of the horse(s) that have been on the lead, controlling the pace.

There is a reason why, all things being equal, a match race featuring a front-runner and a closer never turns out well for the closer.

The best of all the possible worlds for a closer comes to pass when the horse(s) he wishes to reach and get by have been so hard used, their SPEED so decimated, that they commence to decelerate and drift backward into his waiting arms, in which case he has to use that much less of his

SPEED to make up the ground he has ceded in the early going. This occurs, the closer who has benefited is said to have sat the 'garden trip.'

Having listed all the ways in which a closer is disadvantaged, I'll now speak to the virtues of one type of closer, albeit a very special one: a stalker. If the class of the field is a stalker, I'm all in in terms of evaluating his chances.

Because of their versatility, stalkers are more likely to sit the 'garden trip' than any other type of runner.

The manner in which a stalker goes about his or her business is quite similar to those of a front-runner that can rate. The big difference is that a stalker does not have to be on the lead throughout, even though he most probably has enough early foot to do so if that was his goal. Whereas a front-runner that can rate downshifts only after he has taken control of the lead, a stalker downshifts to a lesser gear soon after the break, whereupon he stakes out a position fairly close up behind the leaders, in, well, a stalking position, two or three lengths behind the frontrunners that are battling to take control of the early going.

A stalker's strategy is such that it precludes the front-runner, irrespective of their being the sort that does or doesn't rate, from getting away and putting all sorts of daylight between him and them. A stalker eschews leading from flag fall to a finish, and with it, the early speed duels that might otherwise use up his SPEED, and, in so doing, compromise his chances. I like a stalker, I like him that much more if my analysis suggests that a hotly contested speed duel will take place in front of him. The more intense and obdurate the speed duel that takes place in front of him, the better it is for the stalker, or for that matter, any closer. Because the stalker sits closest to the pace setters than any other closer, he has the least amount of ground to make up, and therefore, of all the closers, he is most enviably positioned. The less ground he has to make up, the less of his SPEED will be used for that task, meaning he will have that much more left of his SPEED with which to do battle if and when he 'hooks' and engages the leaders.

The stalker's strategy or doctrine, if you will, is to break alertly, find a propitious spot, and then, at some strategically appropriate point, tap into his SPEED, fire, and take up after what is hopefully a weakening phalanx of pace setters. Hopefully, for the stalker, the frontrunner who wins the early lead will find his victory to be of the pyrrhic variety, so that he easily succumbs to the stalker's entreaties, surrendering with minimal resistance when the stalker 'hooks' him.

Once the stalker acquires the lead, he then behaves in the same manner as a frontrunner who can rate. Seated firmly in the cat's bird seat, he downshifts to a lesser gear so he will have something left to defend his newly acquired lead should any closers who sit further back, fire, tap into their SPEED, loom, reach him, and offer up a challenge.

A stalker, like all closers, does not mind if he is not in front throughout as long as he is in front at the wire. Relative to front runners, horses, especially stalkers, who come from off the pace are patient sorts capable of biding their time. Their mentality, in a nutshell, is "he who laughs last, laughs hardest."

I think a stalker is the best; the only time I'll have second thoughts about betting on him is if there is just one front-runner in the race, that frontrunner is able to rate, and the disparity in quality between him and the stalker is not all that significant. Such a horse might well be a stalker's downfall, the proverbial fly in the ointment, if he is able to set a slow, uncontested pace of the rocking horse variety.

A front-runner, a horse of lesser quality, wins because he is the lone speed, gets loose on the lead and sets an inordinately slow pace that takes little out of him; he is said to have stolen the race. The best horse gets loose on the lead, sets glacial fractions, and wins for fun; the race hasn't been stolen. He's the best horse. The race was his to do with as he saw fit. He owned it.

Stalkers perform with great efficiency because they possess 'tactical speed.' 'Tactical Speed' is a nice kind of speed to have. It confers all sorts of benefits. It's the main reason why stalkers sit the 'garden trip' more often than any other type of runner. A horse has tactical speed, it means that anywhere, anytime, his SPEED is available, and is there for the asking, and is as easy to access as pressing the remote to change channels. Anytime, anywhere, a horse with 'tactical speed' wishes to tap into his SPEED, he can do so in a heartbeat, which confers all sorts of advantages as it gives him the ability to instantaneously adapt to any tactical exigencies a race might present. Horses with tactical speed are able to take advantage of any window of opportunity, irrespective of the form it might take when and if it presents itself and with it the potential advantage it might proffer. Also, because of the maneuverability with which 'tactical speed' endows a horse, it can help such a horse and his rider to avoid potentially problematic situations, like when a riderless horse is in play, running wild after tossing his jockey at the break.

Tactical speed makes a horse eminently versatile. Whether a horse is versatile because he has tactical speed or he has tactical speed because he is versatile is a 'what came first, a chicken or the egg' kind of conundrum for which I have no answer.

Yet another arrow in a stalker's quiver that makes him such a daunting presence lies in the fact that most stalkers possess more or less the same sort of early speed as a front runner. If he didn't, he couldn't stay as close to the early foot as he does, stalking. So should no early foot assert itself, meaning no true front runners are present, a stalker, should he choose to do so, can easily assume the role of a frontrunner that can rate, bend the pace to his will as is the wont of such runners, and wire the field in the same facile fashion as such a frontrunner would.

I enjoy watching stalkers go about their business. Their approach is so sensible, efficient, and pragmatic that it is difficult not to admire the manner in which they do their thing and accomplish their desired end, winning.

For all the reasons noted, most of the serious bets I make are either on front runners that rate or stalkers.

A frontrunner, whether he can rate or not, gets used up in a duel with similarly minded frontrunners it is a legitimate excuse.

****

The further back from which a horse closes, the more imperative it is that the horses in front of him go at it hammer and tongs and shred each other's chances. If my figuring indicates that the pace the closer, the horse I think best will run into, especially if he is the sort of closer that will come from way back, or worse yet, the clouds, will be of a feeble, dawdling nature, I will not wager on his chances. Not even with bushels of extant Reich Marks from the waning days of the Weimar Republic.

The kind of closer I find myself betting on most often, other than a stalker, is a closer that comes from mid-pack. A closer-situated midpack has far less ground to make up in order to reach the leader(s) than those who come from further back. This means a mid-pack closer gets to use that much less of his SPEED to reach, loom alongside, and 'hook' the horse he seeks to displace.

I rarely bet on a horse who closes from far back, and worse still, from the clouds, unless I think that they are tons the best, and then some. In terms of the pace, so many things have to break just right for such a horse(s) to prevail that I tread with great care when considering their chances, same as if I were tip-toeing across an iced over pond. Such horses rarely, if ever, sit the 'garden trip.'

Again, as I believe it is worth repeating, if the pace is slow and makes no demands on the horses racing in front of him, there is nothing a closer can do to change the narrative. All he or she can do to aid and abet their chances is keep their fingers crossed and hope the stars are aligned in their favor, and the early foot will wreak havoc on one another's chances. This is a lot like relying on the kindness of strangers, which is not the sturdiest, most dependable thing to rely on. I can't think of the last time a complete stranger was nice to me.

A closer runs into a slow pace; it is a legitimate excuse. Unfortunately, next time out, he will most probably encounter the same sort of problem, for which he again will have no solution.

When deciphering the chances of a closer, the distance must be factored in. The shorter the distance, the further back a closer comes from, the harder it is for him to have a positive say in the outcome for the simple reason the race ends all too quickly, and even if he is flying at the leader, his effort might well be rendered null and void for the simple reason that he runs out of ground.

Obviously, it is easier to make up a 10-length deficit at a mile and a half, no matter how slow the pace, than to do so at six furlongs, no matter how fast the fractions set by the pacesetters. This is not to say that there aren't any sprinters, professionals, winners, who come from way back and have productive careers; but still, it's a tough way to make a living.

The further the distance, the less queasy I am about betting a closer. I think a horse is best at a classic distance, I'll bet him that no matter how late in the race he commences his run, even if he comes from the clouds, as there is a lot of both time and ground at his disposal with which to make up the deficit he has ceded in the early going.

Any species of closer reaches and puts away the horse that has been leading; upon acquiring the lead, his role changes. He is no longer the hunter; he's now the hunted. A target, the same as a bull's eye, is now affixed to his back. Another closer then puts him away; he becomes the frontrunner, with the target now affixed to his back, and so it goes, on and on, till the finish line is reached and a winner declared.

When figuring the pace, I always check to see if a 'gate freak' is present. A 'gate freak,' even a cheap one, can cause the best horse grief. A 'gate freak' is denoted as such because he breaks the gate as if shot out of a cannon. Before the others know what hit them, a 'gate freak' can easily put two or three lengths on the field. If the best horse is a frontrunner and he has to deal with a 'gate freak,' it makes his taking control of the early lead that much more arduous as he as to use up that much more of his SPEED in order to make up the ground the 'gate freak' has endowed himself with. A 'gate freak' breaks the gate like the 'gate freak' he is; it is as if the field has been sucker punched, surprised, and caught off guard, ambushed, the same as an unwary stagecoach set upon by highwaymen. A 'gate freak' goes wire to wire; he is said to have 'speed popped' the field.

After identifying the styles in which all the entrants in a race will run, we come to the hard part: figuring out how the various pieces of the puzzle will interact.

As previously touched upon, the most important nugget of information I wish to glean when figuring the pace, what I most want to apprehend, is the status of the horse, I think best 70 or so yards from the wire. Specifically, I want to have a handle on how much of his SPEED he or she still has left relative to the others, where the others will be positioned, and the number, nature, and quality of the challenges they might have to deal with at this critical juncture.

If the horse I think best will run on or near the front, either a frontrunner or a stalker, I try as best I can to get an understanding of how many tussles I anticipate he will engage in, and how much each encounter will take out of him, with an eye toward understanding what he will have left for the endgame as it is played out in the shadow of the wire. I also would like to have an idea at that juncture as to the nature and the quality of the horses in his rearview mirror and which of them, if any, will offer up a serious challenge.

Should I expect the horse I think is best at this critical point to be leg-weary, shortening stride, decelerating, and gasping for air like a guttering flame, or should I expect that he will still be full of run, going easy, with more than enough to see him home a winner?

If the horse I like is one who comes from off the pace and closes on the leaders, I try to come to a meaningful understanding of not only how much of his SPEED he will have left when he reaches those on the lead he is accosting, but also how much the horses he is closing in on will have left in the tank as per the battles they have fought. And if I believe he will prevail and gain the lead, I then calculate his chances the same as if he were now a frontrunner, as that is what he has become, i.e., how much does he have left and what is the status of those who are closing on him in search of the lead? All of which is a lot easier said than done. As noted earlier, figuring the pace is not a day at the beach. Lots of moving parts to consider. Easily the toughest thing one has to come to grips with when trying to figure out if the best horse is good enough to get the job done. It can and will give you headaches.

Lots of times, figuring out the pace becomes so complex, complicated, and convoluted that I feel as if I have wandered into unfathomable labyrinth from which, no matter how hard I try, I will never be able, no matter what, to arrive at the correct solution that will allow me to wend my way clear and again see the light of day.

If, after all of my figuring, if the race appears as if it might well be one of those closely run affairs where the issue might well be determined by a bob of the head, to my way of thinking, it is cutting things just a tad too close, and a serious bet is out of the question.

As to how I go about reaching my opinion as to how much will be taken out of a horse when he is 'hooked up' with another and what they will have left? All I can say is this: after watching horse races for over 60 years, I have no formulas, just my intuition, which I believe isn't half bad.

Even though they are not going to win, 'quitting rats,' 'hanging dogs, 'excuse' horses,' and those afflicted with 'seconditis,' are live pieces, meaning they will at some point bring their SPEED into play, and therefore their exertions must be considered as their efforts, the manner in which they use their SPEED, may well impact the best horse's chances. Just because a horse has no shot at getting to the winner's circle does not mean he cannot affect the outcome. It annoys me no end when the efforts of a horse who is an inveterate loser lays waste to the best horse's chances. It seems to me to be spiteful, mean-spirited, the equine equivalent of schadenfreude, and nothing to be proud of.

If a 'hanging dog,' a rat, or a horse prone to coming in second, or some other type of loser is the horse I think the best horse will have to deal with come crunch time, I am both relieved and elated because if that is the case, there is little cause for worry.

The vast majority of horses run in one particular style. However, there are horses that might run to the front one race, then the next race assumes the persona of a mid-pack closer, etc. I hate to see horses like this in a race where I like a horse, especially if such horses have some quality and can and will affect the outcome, for the simple reason that figuring out how they will impact the pace becomes a bit of a guessing game. I don't like guessing games. Such horses are annoying.

The only occasion when a closer gets to control the race is when his connections run a stablemate, a sacrificial lamb known as a 'rabbit.' The 'rabbit' is not expected to win. The hope is that the 'rabbit's' presence and his early 'speed' will force the horse they believe is the obstacle to their horse winning, a front runner, to use himself up far more than he otherwise would if he was alone on the lead and the 'rabbit' not present.

When a horse's connections send out a 'rabbit,' they invariably attempt to justify their behavior by saying they are doing so to ensure an 'honest' pace, as if by sending the 'rabbit,' they were adding an element of probity to the race it otherwise lacked. Not the way I look at it. When a 'rabbit' is entered, the only message being sent is a tacit admission, a compliment really, that one-on-one the 'rabbit's' entry mate is not good enough to get the job done. No matter, it is an eminently acceptable strategy. I'm sure if I was in a situation where, in order to win a prestigious race, I had to send out a 'rabbit,' I would. What I wouldn't do is say I was ensuring an 'honest' pace.

A horse who throughout his career has raced in one particular style suddenly changes his style, i.e., a mid-pack closer turns into a front runner, a frontrunner into a stalker, etc.; it is called a 'change of action.' Oftentimes, when a horse has a 'change of action,' it ends up meaning nothing, old wine in a new bottle. However, every so often, it does make a difference. Sometimes it is almost as if a new horse emerges Phoenix-like from the ashes of what he previously was and he or she evolves into a new, improved, upgraded version of their former self.

I am especially intrigued when a 'change of action' happens soon after a claim. Obviously, the new trainer knows something the previous trainer did not.

A horse with the requisite intangibles to get the job done evidences a change of action; next time he runs, I pay careful attention.

A brief word about front runners going sprints to routes. When the best horse, a front runner, proceeds to go sprints to routes, stretching out to a distance I know he can handle, I eye the proceedings most carefully, as there might well be an overlay lying in wait, a pot of gold at the end of a rainbow, only that much more accessible.

Let's say last time out, a frontrunner was entered in a sprint replete with front runners who were better and more dominant. As expected, he got chewed up in a speed duel, and was done, toasted, going in the wrong direction at the half mile pole, eventually finishing way in arrears.

Next time out, he is slated to race at a route, a two-turn affair at a mile and $1/16^{th}$, a distance I know he can handle as he has done so in the past. What happens, people look at his last race, see he tired badly at six furlongs, and erroneously reason, if he tired at six furlongs, how can he possibly stay a mile and $1/16^{th}$?

Here's how. The sort of speed required to acquire the lead in a six-furlong sprint is of a much sharper variety than the sort of speed needed to take control of the lead in a route. Asked to go a mile and 1/16th after failing at six furlongs, his speed having been honed by his sprint effort, the horse in question will get the early lead, easy as breaking twigs, set a soft, beneficial pace, go wire to wire, and win for fun. I see the horse I like, a horse I think best going sprints to routes, I have been known to get goosebumps.

Track Biases

In order to figure the pace with any degree of accuracy, the track's biases that are in play must be considered. A track's biases can at times be the key to understanding what will or has already transpired. If the track bias(s) favors the best horse, I like his chances that much more. If it does not, I have to try and figure out if he or she is of sufficient quality to overcome the adversity that the bias(s) will impose.

Figuring out the pace is hard enough. Figuring how the biases on a particular day will impact the pace makes figuring the pace correctly that much more difficult. It's like a juggler adding another ball or two to his routine.

There are two types of bias. One can and will change from day to day, and that is the track's relative ability to tire a horse and, in so doing, use up his SPEED. The other bias is a constant, an absolute that never changes. An invariable, it is a function of how a race is formatted relative to a track's configuration.

A horse loses because of a track bias(s) it's a legitimate excuse.

On days when the track bias(s) overwhelmingly favor the front runners, the speed is said to be 'giant' or 'iron.' On a day when the bias(s) severely mitigate a front runner's chances and enhance those of a closer's, the speed is said to be 'dead.' When no biases are in play, the track is said to be 'honest.' I prefer days when the track is 'honest,' as it requires that much less thinking on my part. The less wear and tear on my brain, the better. My brain, like my knees, has little tread left on the tire. An orthopedic surgeon recently informed me that my knees were like those cities in the rust belt that are desperately in need of new infrastructure.

A racing surface and, with it, its relative ability to tire a horse and use up his SPEED, can easily change from one day to the next. Sometimes dramatically so. The temperature, the moisture, the wind, etc., as well as the manner in which the surface is tended to by the track superintendent, all can have an effect. Consequently, I monitor a surface's biases as vigilantly as I do a horse's form.

There are certain sorts of unfairness that are beyond our understanding, like a horse drowning in the infield lake, a cashier dropping dead, etc. By definition, a track bias is unfair. If, however, one understands the bias and its unfairness, one can turn it to one's advantage.

The less tiring the surface, the better it is for the early speed, as their SPEED will last that much longer before it is 'used up', and the horse in question elides into deceleration mode. And when he does, the manner in which he decelerates will be that much less abrupt. The longer a front runner's SPEED lasts, the less dramatic the ensuing deceleration once his SPEED' is used up, the more difficult it will be for those in pursuit to reach, 'hook' him, and take control of the lead.

The more tiring the surface, the more it favors the closer. The quicker a track uses up a front runner's SPEED, the shorter the distance the frontrunner will be able to get before he is 'used up' and commences to decelerate. Which in turn means those closers in pursuit will have that much less ground to make up in order to reach the horse with whom they intend to vie with for the lead. And when said closer does reach and engage his target, the horse on the lead he is seeking to supplant will have that much less SPEED with which to fight off his advances. In addition, the more tiring the track, the more dramatic the leader's subsequent deceleration will be, making it that much easier for any closer in ardent pursuit to reach, 'hook,' and put him away.

A front-runner wants his SPEED to last as long as possible. On a day when the track is 'dead,' when it sucks the SPEED out of a frontrunner as quick as an ice cube melts on a red hot griddle, whatever inherent advantage setting the pace confers to a horse on the lead is severely compromised.

To understand how one surface can be more tiring than another, how it can impact how long a horse's SPEED will carry him, and what will come to pass when he can longer accelerate, I propose the following experiment. Go to the beach. Walk to the water's edge, where the foam from the breaking waves washes up on the sand. The sand there is dark, moist, and offers firm footing. Feel it. Take its measure. It's firm and compact, and doesn't slip or slide beneath your feet. It affords excellent purchase, ideal leverage from which to push off. Draw a line in the sand. Imagine that line is a starting gate and you're a stone-cold frontrunner that doesn't rate. From a standing start, bring your SPEED into play just as such a frontrunner would when the starting gate clangs open, and run as fast as you can for as long as you can along the dark, damp strip of sand that runs like a ribbon between sand and sea. When you reach that point at which you're 'used up' and can no longer accelerate, the point where you begin to decelerate, draw an X.

Now walk back to where you started. Upon reaching the line that served as your make believe starting gate, turn and walk perpendicular from the water's edge to the middle of the beach, where the sand, untouched by seawater, is hot, deep, loose, and slips and slides underfoot, affording little to any traction. Again, draw a line to represent a starting gate, and again use your SPEED to sprint as fast as you can for as long as you can parallel to the line you took when you raced along the shoreline. When you are used up and begin to decelerate, mark the spot with an X. Compare the two exes. I guarantee that the X that you drew on the shoreline will be much further ahead of the X marking the spot on the sand when you sprinted mid-beach as your SPEED along the less tiring shoreline lasted that much longer. Not only that, when you decelerated there, it was significantly less abrupt than when you did so on the hot, dry, loose sand that had been baking mid beach.

Which surface would you prefer to compete on if you had a frontrunners' skill set? Not even close. The glib surface along the shore that enhanced your stamina and allowed you to carry your speed that much further. Not only that but when you were 'used up' and began to decelerate, it was nowhere near as dramatic as when you decelerated on the hot, loose sand in the middle of the beach.

If you were closer and were asked to choose the medium best suited to your racing style, the one that gave you the best chance of winning, the moist, damp sand at the waterline or the dry, loose sand in the middle of the beach, you would most certainly select the latter as it would make your task of catching and getting by the horse(s) in front of you that much easier. Not only would you reach them sooner, their SPEED having been used up that much earlier, the horse(s) in front of you would be decelerating that much more dramatically, coming back to you that much quicker, and having in hand that much less energy with which to turn back your entreaties when you 'hooked' them and battle was joined.

In summation, the glibber the track, the better it is for the early speed. The more tiring the track, the better it is for a closer.

I've seen days where the track was so biased in favor of the speed, the speed so 'giant,' the going so easy, that whichever frontrunner took command early went wire to wire and won for fun. Days when the 'early foot' appeared capable of going on forever and forever and then some.

Generally speaking, the wetter and more sodden a dirt surface is, the more strongly it is biased in favor of the 'speed,' provided, of course, the 'speed' can handle the footing on an off track. Sloppy tracks use the front runners' SPEED nary at all. Pacesetters skip along it in effortless fashion same as scudding clouds on a windy day.

One would think that on a day where the track was sloppy, locating winners would be easy. Find a dominant frontrunner that loves the slop and let the bias do the rest.

As previously noted, I wish that life was that easy. It's not. I have seen so many inexplicable results transpire on wet tracks, so many seemingly unbeatable 'mortal locks' bested by improbable sorts, that I make sure to stay home when it is raining.

I know my weaknesses, my soft spots. At times, I'm a perfect example of what Oscar Wilde was referring to when he said, "The only thing I can't resist is temptation." By staying home on rainy days, I keep whatever invidious temptations the races might offer that day well beyond my reach.

And then there are those days when the speed, no matter its quality, has no chance. None! Days that as soon as a horse brings his SPEED into play, he's used up in the blink of an eye, and is left staggering, gasping for air as if stricken by a coronary. The sort of day that is so biased in favor of closers that horses closing from the clouds inherit the lead as if by default, race after race as if it were their birthright.

The reason horses that come from the clouds enjoy such success on such days is that they are the last ones to fire. Thus, they are the last to bring their SPEED into play over the tiring surface that has sucked the life out of every horse that has 'fired' before them. As a horse closing from the clouds is the last horse to bring his SPEED into play, he wins by default, as he's the last man standing. On such a day, I like a late closer, I like him that much more. On such days, I have even been known to bet on horses that came from the 'clouds,' in sprints no less.

How then does one go about ascertaining whether a surface is biased, in whose favor, and to what degree? The best way I know of is to take note of how reliable professional, legitimate horses, especially frontrunners, are faring. A real deal sort of a frontrunner who knows how to get the job done, gets an easy lead, sets beneficial fractions, and then runs out of gas at the 1/8th pole for no apparent reason, and then the same sort of thing happens in the next race as well; what am I to think other than the track is tiring and is biased against those who are into displaying 'early foot'.

In the first race of the day, a frontrunner who is clearly not the best horse, not even in the conversation, gains an early lead, then turns back one or more legitimate stalkers, a mid-pack closer or two, and draws off to win in a gallop. I am left with no other alternative but to think that the surface is biased in favor of pace setters. The pattern persists, I pretty much know for certain that the speed is 'iron.'

Another sure sign that the speed is 'giant' is if a frontrunner that is usually on empty and gasping for air at the 1/2 mile pole is hard used early, holds the lead to the quarter pole, and then when he straightens for home, accelerates, 'rebreaks,' draws off, and wins. On a day when stuff like that is happening, no matter how much I like a closer, even if he's a stalker that runs close to the pace, I will think twice and then some before I invest in his chances.

Cheap speed loses, goes backward, it means nothing because that's what cheap speed does. Cheap speed not only wins but keeps winning and, in the process, overcomes all sorts of adversity I am being informed in no uncertain terms that investing in horses that come from off the pace is a poor approach.

At the other extreme, if first race or two closers of minimal talent, who never run by anyone, save if the horse in front of them has broken down and lies inert on the track, suddenly storm past a slew of legitimate sorts racing in front of them, acquire the lead, and actually hold on to win, I commence to focus on those who do their best running from off the pace, as what else am I to think other than being in front early is not the place to be.

I also take note of what transpires in the stretch. Do legitimate sorts attempting to close on the leaders, though they seem as if they are giving their all, appear to be running in place, as if on a treadmill, unable to gain an inch? If such is the case, the surface is telling me it's not very tiring, as none of the horses that are racing forwardly are decelerating and drifting back to the field.

On the other hand, come the stretch, if those doing the closing are all gobbling up huge swatches of ground and surging like a wave past those who had raced on or near the lead, I know the speed is in dire straits and not to be bet on. The reason the speed is coming back to those closing, dying en masse, the same as the dinosaurs did when the asteroid hit, is because the track, quite tiring, has sucked so much out of them, it is causing them to drift backward like sailboats buffeted by a strong headwind. I see a stretch drive or two where that happens, I commence to look at a frontrunner's chances with a somewhat jaundiced eye.

Yet another rule of thumb, the fewer position changes that occur during the course of the race, the more likely it is that the surface is glib. The field breaks, the contestants assume their positions, and then go around the track as if on parade with none of the participants able to either gain or lose ground, it generally means that no one is decelerating; ergo, the racing surface isn't very tiring.

Lots of changes in position indicate to me just the opposite: that the track is tiring. When there is a plethora of lead changes and horses are constantly changing positions, it is pretty safe to assume that the surface is more than just a tad tiring.

The more horses run to form, the less likely it is that a bias is in play. A pattern of abnormalities commences, the first question I ask involves the equity of the surface.

Some days the bias is so egregious that after two or three races, even the dullest and most myopic of observers can't help but be aware of its impact. Most days, though, the bias is anything but obvious, neither black nor white, more of a muddle of gray that takes a bit of pondering before its nature is revealed. Eventually, if you haven't been smoking too much dope with the Rastafarians in the stairwell, the bias, if there is one, should come into focus. If the bias isn't overly apparent, and it is not readily giving up its secrets, and you find yourself straining to apprehend it, the track is probably honest. Sometimes, when figuring, less is more.

No one rolls better blunts than a Rasta. If rolling blunts was an Olympic event, Rastas would win Gold, Silver, and Bronze. They would more than hold their own in the compulsories, and afterward, in the free style portion of the event blow the competition away and dazzle the judges with both the quality of their design and their manual dexterity. Not many people are capable of rolling a perfectly proportioned blunt with one hand while holding and scrutinizing the Racing Form with the other.

It is imperative that one understands that there is no correlation between how a surface is officially labeled by the Stewards, and its ability to tire a horse. Not only are the designations useless in this regard; in fact, they can at times steer a bettor in the wrong direction. I've seen tracks designated slow where the speed was 'immortal,' and tracks labeled fast where a horse's speed withered and died a nanosecond or two after it was brought into play. It would be far more helpful to the public if, in addition to labeling surfaces as Fast, Slow, Sloppy, Good, Muddy, etc., the powers that be were able to accurately designate a surface as either Very Tiring, Tiring, Honest, Not Tiring and Not Tiring Much at All. In the meantime, the best approach; let the racetrack speak for itself.

There are additional biases within the surface's overall biases, biases nesting within biases, that must be taken into account as they can be the key. What I'm referring to is the different lanes in which horses race. The same day the rail might be 'iron,' the outside might be dead, a certified graveyard for any horse with the bad luck to be situated there, or vice versa.

I think the best horse will be forced to run in a lane that is unduly biased against him. I won't bet.

As to why different paths play differently on the same day, I have no idea. Talk to the track superintendent. I simply play the hand I'm dealt.

If race after race horses on the rail are going wire to wire as if on a conveyor belt, the inside is 'iron.' If race after race closers are coming over the top and flying to victory over those inside of them, I know the outside lanes are 'giant,' the place to be. It's not rocket science.

A clue as to how the different lanes are playing can be gathered by taking note as to where the jockeys try to position their mounts. If race after race the riders on the inside seem desperate to take their mounts off and away from the rail, I have to assume the inside is dead and not the place to be. Race after race, I see that the riders are trying to drop their charges to the inside. I assume that the outside is not offering up the best of racing environments.

'Rats' and 'quitting dogs' also can offer clues. A 'rat' or a 'quitting dog' wins I always try to suss how and why such an astonishing result came to pass. Two 'rats' in a row go wire to wire hugging the rail and actually win, a jaw-dropping result; what else am I to think, but the speed is 'giant.' A 'hanging dog' comes flying over the top and easily runs past a legitimate sort who has had it all his own way hugging the rail, the track is telling me in no uncertain terms the inside is tiring.

If horses are running to form, if nothing strange and untoward is happening, it is a good indication that the track is 'honest' and that no biases are in play. Like a scientific experiment, it's the odd result, the abnormality, that demands clarification and explanation, which is why I take special issue with trying to understand what's going on when such a situation comes to pass. A 'rat' or a 'quitting dog' wins, or if a horse comes from the clouds and wins a sprint, it is apparent that an inquiry is required, and the Executive Racing Committee (ERC) is convened on site, at the racetrack, to ponder and come to grips with the situation at hand.

On any given day, the ability of the dirt and turf to tire a horse and use up his SPEED can be polar opposites. To assume that because the speed is 'giant' on the dirt, it will also be 'giant' on the turf is a huge mistake. The fact of the matter is that they most likely will be diametrically opposed.

The best way of figuring out the turf's bias, if indeed there is one, is the same way one goes about figuring out the bias on the dirt. Watch the professionals, especially the frontrunners, to see how their SPEED fares and the patterns that unfold.

The turf's ability to tire a horse is a function of how moist it is, the opposite of that which transpires on the dirt. The drier and firmer the turf, the better it is for the speed. I go to the track in mid-July, and it hasn't rained in two weeks, and the turf is like concrete. I know that the speed on the grass will be 'giant.'

The wetter the grass, the more tiring it is, for the simple reason that a horse's hooves dig deeper into the sod the wetter the surface. The deeper a horse's foot sinks in, the more energy is required for him to then pluck his foot free so he can continue on his way.

To get a sense of what it is like to run on a rain-soaked, soft turf, go run across a wet, boggy meadow. The plucking of one's feet from the muck with each and every stride will, in terms of your energies, most certainly take its toll.

I only bet on the turf if it's Fast, Firm, or Good. I've seen too many other unworldly results come to pass on Soft or Yielding turf courses for me to hazard a bet on such enigmatic surfaces. I've learned the hard way, same as I've learned most of the lessons that life has hammered into me.

Then there are those biases that are immutable and always in play. These biases are predicated on a track's configuration and how a race is formatted as per the distance. Once you know these biases, you will always know them, as they're invariables that never change. After a while, you simply take them into account with little to no reflection, like taking a breath or blinking your eyes.

There are two innate biases. One is a function of the sharpness of a racetrack's turns; the other is the distance from the starting gate to the first turn. The tighter the turn, the shorter the run into the first turn, the better it is for those who use their speed early. The wider the turn, the longer the run into the first turn, the less of an advantage will accrue to a frontrunner.

The first runner into a turn is accorded an advantage because he saves all the ground. The sharper and more hairpin the first turn, the better it is for the horse who reaches it first, as those racing in arrears of him will be forced to run wider, condemning them to covering that much more ground. A two-turn race amplifies the benefit twofold.

To even the playing field and alleviate the bias that the first runner into a tight first turn enjoys, in men's and women's track and field, both indoors and outdoors, in 200 and 400 meter races, the contestants run in staggered lanes throughout the event so all the contestants run the same distance. If the lanes weren't staggered, the runner in lane one would run 200 meters, and the runner stuck out in lane eight would run maybe 220 meters. That wouldn't be very fair, now would it?

Thoroughbreds do not race in staggered lanes. If a horse is stuck on the outside, that's life in the big city, and what are you going to do? I always told my children when something irked them, life's not always fair; get over it.

To illustrate, let's look first at a mile race on what used to be Aqueduct's Inner Dirt track. Like one of those nested Russian Dolls, the inner-dirt track sat inside the turf course, which in turn sat inside Aqueduct's mile and 1/8th main track. The turns on the Inner Dirt were the sharpest turns to be found at any major, big-time venue. At a mile, the starting gate was positioned about 70 or so yards from the first turn. The run into the first turn was so abbreviated that whoever had the highest turn of 'early foot' was assured to be first into the turn, and so doing, gain a huge advantage over the others. It was almost as if such a horse were being given a head start. Then, after a relatively short run along the back stretch, the stretch turn would come into play, and the horse on the lead would then be able to save that much more ground, further leveraging the advantage he was given on the clubhouse turn. I thought a horse best, knew he could stay a mile, that he liked the inner dirt, that the track was glib, and that he had the speed to get into the clubhouse turn first, I knew I liked his chances more than just an awful lot.

Let's now look at and compare a mile on the now defunct Inner-Dirt at the Big A to a mile at Belmont. Though both are at a mile, for all practical purposes, they are two completely different races. Whatever advantages a mile on the inner dirt afforded a frontrunner are more or less absent at Belmont, moot points.

With its mile-and-a-half circumference, Belmont is the biggest track in N. America. It also has the widest, most sweeping turns of any track as well. Being first into the first turn at Belmont doesn't mean all that much. It's nice, but no big deal, certainly not the advantage that the 'early foot' would be in receipt of when they are first into the turn on the inner dirt.

Also, at a mile at Belmont, the run into the first turn is a half-mile straightaway run out of the chute, compared to 70 or so yards on the inner dirt. On the inner dirt, a frontrunner had only to use his SPEED for 70 yards in order to gain the lead and be first into the Clubhouse turn and the advantage that comes with it. Not so at Belmont. To get into the first turn first at a mile, a frontrunner at Belmont has to use a lot more of his SPEED because, after breaking the gate, he has to race a half mile down a straightaway before the first turn is reached.

Finally, at Belmont, a mile is a one-turn affair. Whatever advantage a turn offers at Belmont, minimal as it is, it only happens once, as opposed to a mile on the inner dirt where there are two sharp turns, each biased big time in favor of the horse that reaches the turns first.

I have neither the time nor the inclination to list which distances at which race tracks benefit frontrunners and to what degree. You do that. Simple formula: the tighter the turn, the shorter the run into the first turn, the better it is for a front runner.

In order to come to an understanding of the 'bias,' if any, that's operating on a particular day, we have to wed what we know about those biases that are variable, like how tiring the surface is, with those immutable biases which are dictated by how the race is formatted. If a race is scheduled for a mile and a sixteenth on Aqueduct's main track, a two-turn event with a short run into the first turn, and the surface is glib, the benefit to the pace setters increases accordingly. On the other hand, same horse, same field, same distance, only the race is at Belmont, a one-turn affair with a 9/16th of a mile run from the starting gate out of a chute down a straightaway before the first turn is reached, and the surface is tiring, the frontrunner that was a 'lock' at Aqueduct could be summarily written off as having no shot at all.

Sometimes the biases are at cross purposes. Like the track is dead, but the race is at a mile and 70 yards at Finger Lakes, or the track is glib, but the race is carded for a mile and an eighth at Belmont, with a five-furlong run out of a chute and down a straightaway into one wide, sweeping turn. It can get tricky.

There is one other bias: the wind. I don't factor the wind into the equation all that often. Only when it is especially rambunctious and blowing real hard. As a general rule, the stronger the wind is blowing into the faces of the front runners, the better it is for those who will close. Battling strong winds can use up a horse on the lead, the same as struggling with a headwind can cause a plane to use up that much more gas and be late to arrive at its destination. On days when the wind is blowing hard at a frontrunner's back, I like their chances that much more as it is like an aircraft getting pushed along by the jet stream. The plane gets there quicker using that much less gas.

When a horse wins when the track biases are profoundly antithetical to his doing so, he or she catches my attention. One example comes to mind. It had been raining for several days. Aqueduct's inner dirt track was like soup. Usually on such a day, I stay home, but I went to the track just to hang out. The early speed was 'immortal.' Rats were winning, going wire-to-wire. Whichever horse led at the top of the stretch drew off and won. At no point during the day did any closer, no matter their quality, have any impact. In the feature race, there was a legitimate, hard-knocking, professional sort with a dazzling burst of early, 'gate freak' like speed. He loved a sloppy track as well as six furlongs on the Inner Dirt. He was in career form. He went off 1–5. In the same race, there was a three-year-old colt who had raced two or three times but whom I had never heard of. At the top of the stretch, the favorite was five lengths to the good. The race, or so it appeared, was over, history. However, as the field commenced to straighten for home, the lightly raced three-year-old, racing widest of all no less, was maybe six or seven lengths off the lead. But then he 'fired' and brought into play a move that can only be described as being of the jet-propelled variety. He gobbled up ground at a prodigious rate, swooshed on by the horse on the lead like that one was standing still, and drew off under a hand ride, the easiest of winners. He got my attention and then some. Convinced that I had seen the real deal, as soon as I got home, I called a meeting of the Executive Racing Committee (ERC). It was a closed door meeting. I argued for a waiver that would allow me to bet on the lightly raced three-year-old that had won that afternoon. The waiver was granted with minimal debate. I ended up betting the colt next time out, and next time after that, and so forth and so on, culminating with that three-year-old colt upsetting Spectacular Bid, who was 1–9 in the Belmont Stakes, ending Spectacular Bid's quest to be a Triple Crown winner. The colt's name was Coastal. It's not often you see a horse laugh in the face of adversity, but when you do, it is a good idea to take note. I made a lot of money with Coastal. He was like an annuity.

Form

Time ceaselessly meanders, rambles, and races through the cracks and crevices of the universe. Stars are born, light up the void for eons, then collapse into singularities from which nothing escapes. Particles leap into existence for a nanosecond or two and then just as abruptly subside and disappear back into the flux from which they arose. Mountains rise, erode, then slowly disappear, and dissolve into nothingness as if they were never more than a fiction in someone's imagination. We live. We die. Seasons change. Leaves wither and fall. A thoroughbred's form and his ability to compete is no different. It can and will change. It's the last box on my list that I need to check in the affirmative before I will make my way to the windows.

If I'm going to lose, it's not going to be because the horse I fancy is unwilling or unable to fire his best shot. I'll only bet on the horse I think best if I believe he is in good form, sitting on ready, and is able to bring his A-game to the proceedings.

Professionals that meet all the criteria on my ready list, including having their A game in hand, are not all that plentiful. It's Friday morning. I just finished breakfast, a blueberry muffin, and a cup of tea. I'm perusing The Racing

Form, prospecting for situations I might wish to invest in. Nine tracks, 87 races; 765 horses slated to compete.

Of the 765 horses entered today, I consider only 31 of them to be legitimate sorts who sport the intangibles that I so value. The type of horse on whom I will consider making a wager on if I think he or she is the best and all the conditions as per my check list are being met. And of the 31, only 19 are enjoying, in my opinion, sufficiently good form to warrant a bet.

This does not mean I am going to bet on the nineteen. It just means that the nineteen are under serious consideration. The nineteen are entered in 13 of the 87 races carded. Rest assured, I will view all 13 races. How else can I keep tabs on the form of the 31 horses I respect? Every race is a learning experience. A tidbit here, a tidbit there, eventually, hopefully, it all adds up. As for the vast majority of races carded today, I pay them no heed. Checking out the performance of horses I have no interest in is not a good use of my time.

The best way to assess a horse's physical form is by acquainting yourself with the current state of his most potent weapon, his speed. When a horse is in his best form, his speed is at its most compelling, and he is able to accelerate as quickly and efficiently as a well-tuned sports car. The more moves a horse can bring into play, the more lethal and daunting they are, the better his physical form. The fewer gears a horse has at his disposal, the less intimidating and menacing they are, the more one can rest assured that his best form has absconded and left him in the lurch.

Perhaps today, in one or more of the 13 races, a critical nugget of information will be secured. For example, a professional sort who has been dreadful of late unleashes a burst of speed that is reminiscent of the sort he displayed when he was a force to be reckoned with. It might well be a none-too-subtle indication that perhaps he is finding his best form and I should seriously vet his chances next time he or she is entered. On the other hand, if a legitimate sort who has been on a tear comes up empty, it might well be a sign that his form has commenced to deteriorate.

A word about what I consider to be a key race. A key race is one that contains multiple horses, all of whom are manifesting good form, all of whom are legitimate sorts more than capable of winning if given a reasonable opportunity to do so. Today, five of the 19 horses that have checked all the boxes on my ready list, including having their A form, are scheduled to compete in the same race, a turf affair at the Fair Grounds. Five professionals, all with a license to win, thus a key race. Obviously, only one will make his way to the winner's circle. However, the four horses that will have lost will all have a legitimate excuse. The excuse being that they were beaten fair and square by a professional, real-deal racehorse horse who brought his A game to the table. Rest assured that next time any of those four horses race, as they have in hand a legitimate excuse, I will be on high alert and parse their chances with a fine-tooth comb. Not only will I be eminently conversant with why they lost, but I will also have in my possession the most current data as to their current form. Also, next time they race, no matter the nature of the loss, but simply because they lost, their odds will most likely have about them the sweet smell of an overlay.

I am always alert to any indication that a horse I consider a professional sort is on the cusp of finding his or her best form. The sooner I am made aware that next time a horse on my radar is going to most probably show his best form, the sooner I will be able to jump on his bandwagon. The longer it takes one to hop on board a horse's bandwagon, the less likely it is that one will get to feast on the overlays that are generated when that runner is first making a statement as to the righteousness of his current form. After a horse has put in a few monster efforts, everybody and his mother will be aware he is currently running holes in the wind, and the pay-offs he engenders will become somewhat less inspiring. The pay-offs that a horse brings to the table when he is at the end of a winning streak are somewhat anemic, nowhere as juicy when compared to those produced when he first elided into juggernaut mode.

As important as it is to know when to jump on a horse's bandwagon, it is just as important to know when to jump off. The sooner you realize a horse's form is deteriorating, the less likely it is that your bankroll will be impacted by cash flow problems. Make one bet too many on a horse whose best form is in remission, and you can easily give back all the money you made betting on him or her when they were firing on all cylinders.

I try to keep tabs on my form as a handicapper as assiduously as I keep tabs on the form of the horses on my radar. Every time I bet, I'm betting on myself, on the rectitude and prescience of my opinion. My form in this regard comes and goes. Sometimes I'm sharp as can be, and every decision I make is spot on. And then there are those times when my chances of coming up with a winner are on a par with a dead piece winning. As to why my form changes and it can happen overnight, I have no idea. I have thought a lot as to why my form changes, and to date, the only conclusion I've come to is that somewhere out there in the vast and foreboding darkness of the universe, there is a fuse with my name on it, and every so often it is in need of replacing. The best remedy when I'm stuck in the quicksand of a slump is for me to take a few days off and freshen myself, just as a horse's connections would if a horse of theirs had gone a bit sour. Eventually, hopefully, sooner than later, I'll regain my winning form. Why? Clearly, someone or something reached out and replaced the fuse that had shorted out, the one with my name on it. What other explanation makes sense?

✲✲✲✲✲✲✲✲✲✲✲✲✲✲✲✲✲✲✲✲✲✲✲✲✲

A horse's career is a series of campaigns. Each campaign is a series of races. When a horse returns to the races after a three or more-month hiatus, I view it as the commencement of a new campaign. The three months are an arbitrary construct. Why three months? No other reason other than that it works for me. I find it a productive way of looking at things.

If one were to plot a graph of a prototypical campaign, it would resemble a Bell Curve. The first data points, the races at the start of the campaign, would ascend on the left-hand side of the curve in somewhat orderly fashion as the individual races himself into shape, as, hopefully, he seeks his best form. Then at some point, his best form is realized, the curve's apogee is reached, and he or she is at their best.

Then eventually, inevitably, the rigors of a campaign will use a horse up the same way a horse's SPEED gets used up during the course of a race. Whereupon a horse's form deteriorates, the potency of his moves diminish, and the data points representing his efforts commence to trend downward on the right-hand side of the curve until they fall off the chart. And then, when a horse's form evaporates to such an extent that it borders on the pointless to race him, he or she is taken out of circulation, rested, and freshened until it is determined that he or she can begin training for their next campaign.

Bear in mind, though, that just because a horse is in peak form does not mean victory is guaranteed. Other factors are in play. Like he is competing against foes who are also in fine form. He is entered at a distance or on a surface that he doesn't care for. Or the manner in which the pace unfolds is not in his best interests.

As a general rule of thumb, the more quality a horse has, the more likely it is that he will be able to put together a considerable skein of peak efforts where he is able to bring his A game to the party. The cheaper the horse, the less top-notch efforts he will be able to put forth, maybe only one. A cheap horse, let's say a $5,000 claimer, puts in two or three strong efforts. I become quite leery as I wait for the other shoe to fall. This is not to say such horses can't lay down five or six strong races in a row, but it's certainly not to be counted on.

One of the worst things a horse player can do is dwell in the past, on what previously was. When assessing a horse's current form and how the horse under consideration is most likely to perform next time he races, it is eminently sensible to give the greatest credence and importance to his most recent effort(s). I would think that it goes without saying that the more recent the race, the greater its relevance. Clearly, a race that took place last week tells me more about a horse's current form than an effort that took place six months ago. When attempting to plot a horse's form, where the next data point will land on the graph of his current campaign, I think it is best to use his most recent races as the primary jumping off points.

A horse's moves, especially his speed, or lack thereof, are the best indication as to the state of his physical form, which is why they are the most important factor to be considered when structuring the contours of the Bell Curve his form is etching.

The above-noted model of a typical campaign is just that, a model, and a broad one at that; no more than a context to help one commence deliberations. I've seen campaigns that commenced with a horse being in peak form, after which his form steadily spiraled downward into oblivion. Campaigns where a horse did nothing race after race, whereupon out of the blue he came up with an unexpected 'monster effort,' and then, the very next race, he fell back into the ignominy in which he had previously dwelt. In terms of horse's form, one Bell curve does not fit all.

Yet another rule of thumb: the trajectory of a horse's career mimics the bell-shaped curve of a campaign. The apex of the curve, when a horse is most likely to show his best form, have his best campaigns, occurs between the Autumn of his three-year-old campaign through his fourth, fifth, and sixth years. A horse turns seven years old; he's usually on the downside. Chances are, he will never be as good as he was earlier in his career.

There are countless exceptions. I simply use this very general way of looking at things to give me perspective so I might better anticipate the level of competence I might reasonably expect a horse to display when he commences a new campaign. It helps me manage my expectations. For example, I wouldn't expect a seasoned warrior, a nine-year-old with 60 or more races under his belt upon commencing a new campaign after a four-month hiatus, to sport the sort of form he did when he was four, five, or six.

I am not saying not to bet on a horse when he is on the downward slope of his career. As long as a horse still has the intangibles I so value, I'll bet on him as long as he is in a spot where he meets all the requirements as per my check list.

It is one of the Executive Racing Committee's (ERC) key doctrines to never bet on a horse to do something he has not already done. Driven by this more or less ironclad prescription, I will not conclude a horse is in good form during the course of a campaign till he shows me via his moves that he has either found good form or is clearly on the cusp of doing so. I don't care how brilliant a horse has been in previous campaigns. Every campaign is a new chapter, and before I bet on a horse in the newest chapter which he is writing as to who and what he is, he has to show me he or she is in possession of winning form. Now is now, not yesterday. How a horse performed in earlier campaigns can and will color my expectations, but that's about it. I've seen many horses that throughout their career had one winning campaign after another and who always at some point in a campaign showed good form and then, for whatever reason, the next campaign ran like a 'dead piece,' never showed anything, and appeared to show minimal interest in the proceedings. It happens. No matter how good or how awesome a horse is, eventually, his career comes to a close, and one can only hope he or she enjoys their retirement, especially if it was well earned.

On rare occasions, I will violate my maxim and bet a horse in his first race of a new campaign. According to the Executive Racing Committee (ERC) two criteria must be met: the horse has to have all sorts of quality, and his trainer has to have shown me in the past that when he has such a horse in his barn, he will only race him if he believes his charge is sitting on dead ready and is more than capable of showing winning form at first asking. For many elite trainers, those that manage the fortunes of the best of the best, having their charge show well after a hiatus appears to be a matter of pride, a way of making a statement as to their acumen, their horsemanship, and the extent to which they have mastered their craft. As for those trainers that are able to do so, you figure it out.

Every so often, a horse that has never given me any reason to pay him any heed and whom I had always viewed as an afterthought, filler, if you will, not only begins to exhibit potent moves but also the intangibles I so value. In other words, he turns into a force to be reckoned with, the sort whose fortunes I will now assiduously fellow. As to why this transformation, I have no idea. Maybe, like some people, he's simply a late bloomer, and it just took him that much longer to mature, figure it all out, and get the hang of the game, which is winning. Usually, when such a switch is flipped and the light is turned on, such horses will then evidence those intangibles until their racing days are over. Unless, of course, they don't.

A professional sort who has been showing excellent form shows up empty, bereft of any meaningful moves, it could well be a red flag that his form is waning. Or it could simply be an aberration. Just one of those days. Maybe he had a headache, or something on his mind had become a nagging distraction. Perhaps he simply preferred, rather than race that day, to hang out in the barn with his stablemates and munch hay. Next time he races, I'll adopt a wait-and-see approach. If the next time he races he 'fires' and puts in one of his usual professional efforts, I have no choice but to put his previously uninspired effort down to just one of those days. Shit happens. Even Sandy Koufax had his off days when his fastball lacked its customary 'hop' and his curveball hung like a 'hanging dog' and lacked its usual bite.

A horse shows his best moves yet loses, it means that his physical form is not the issue. The key to his poor effort lies elsewhere. And a legitimate excuse is probably in play. Correctly locate the legitimate excuse, the key that cost him, like the distance, the competition, the pace, or the surface, and if next time out the variable that caused him to falter is not in play, a ticket with your name on it might well be waiting to be cashed.

****

Oftentimes, when a horse begins to lose his form, his connections seek to compensate by dropping him down to meet horses of lesser quality. The rationale being that even though their charge is not in stellar form and has only his B game in hand, if you will, it will be more than sufficient to handle the A game of horses of supposedly lesser quality. Such a move is referred to as a 'drop-down.' Sometimes a 'drop down' wins. Sometimes they do not. I'm not what you would call a 'drop-down' enthusiast. The way I see it, the horse 'dropping down' is going in the wrong direction, and his connection's confidence in him is waning. Oftentimes, 'drop down' is a euphemism for fire sale.

As a former businessman, if someone offered to sell me an asset for $10,000 that the previous week had a valuation of $35,000, a caution flag would run up a flagpole in my brain and wave about frantically, as if pummeled by hurricane winds. Perhaps dropping a horse down is just what the Doctor ordered. Or just the first layer through which the horse will descend on what might well be an inexorable journey to irrelevance.

The other day I saw a horse run for a $3,500 claiming tag at a decidedly third-rate venue. He lost badly. He was never in contention. Three years ago, he was one of the top sprinters in the country. He was a big favorite of mine. A tough, top-of-the-line, hard-knocking sort who always tried as hard as he could. His efforts, if one could say this about a horse's races, had panache. His moves were of the awe-inspiring variety. He was precisely the kind of horse I respect to the nth degree and hold in the highest regard. Also, I cashed a lot of tickets with his name on them. He won a few Grade I Stakes. He was top-notch. Then something happened. He lost it. Overnight, he was a different kind of horse. Happened just like that. Looking to make the best of a bad situation, seeking to salvage something, his connections kept dropping and dropping him down in search of a winning spot. He changed hands several times. He lost and lost and lost, no matter the level at which he was entered. He was a gelding with no breeding value. Obviously, he was still sound, so whoever had him in their barn just kept racing him in the hope his form might regain just a touch of its former luster. Luckily, the first time he was dropped down, I had a vibe, a bad one, and I jumped off his bandwagon. I can only imagine the losses suffered by those who kept betting on him throughout his long slide into infamy. Doubling down each time, each time hoping to win back what they had already lost, is a bad trap to fall into. Eventually, he broke down and was euthanized. He deserved better. Shame on his various owners for not pensioning him off.

The only time I will seriously consider betting on a 'drop down' is if the horse's connections had become overly ambitious, as a horse's connections are wont to be, and they spotted the horse where he was out of his element and he showed nothing. Having learned their lesson, next start, his connections return him to where he belongs. He gets my attention because he's not really dropping down; he's simply back where he belongs. Big difference.

A horse loses his form, I prefer it to be both egregious and abrupt. That way, I know exactly where I stand. The less ambiguity and nebulousness I encounter at the race track, the better off I am. A horse loses his form, I want it to be like Humpty Dumpty when he toppled from his perch and splattered into countless pieces. Then and there, everyone in attendance knew that it was all over for Humpty Dumpty, and even though all the King's horses and all the King's men were called on to put Humpty Dumpty back together again, it was never going to happen. It was all over for Humpty Dumpty, same as a horse that has shattered his sesamoid.

I value loyalty, I really do. That being said, no matter how good a horse has been to me, as soon as he loses his form, I stay away. I might, out of respect, make a two-dollar bet for old-time's sake. But that's it. When I shun a horse I really liked, respected, and had made money with, I feel a bit like a fair-weather friend. Still, I find feeling like a fair-weather friend a lot better than feeling like a loser. It's my belief that the end result of making bets based on nostalgia will find you asking friends to loan you money so you can pay the tolls to get home. The road to hell is paved with good intentions, one of which is betting with your heart instead of your head.

****

A horse's mental conformation does not change anywhere near as often as his physical form. A horse has 'winning ways,' he will most likely exhibit them throughout his career. However, as with everything, there are exceptions. Every so often, a horse that has shown exemplary 'winning ways' throughout his career suddenly behaves in such a manner that one is left with no other option than to believe he or she is no longer in possession of such motivations. Even though the horse's moves remain potent, an indication that his or her physical form is not the issue, the fight and the fire that once animated him, the overweening need to be on the lead at the finish appears to have been snuffed out. How does this happen? I have no idea. If I am ever able to converse with such a horse and I can get him to talk to me as if I were his shrink and he were my patient, I'd delve into his motivations, his formative years, his feelings, and the relationship he had with his dam and sire. But I can't. In my experience, the older a horse is when such a change of heart occurs, this less likely it is that he will ever reach back to his glory years and redeem the intangibles he once possessed.

Much of my sense that a horse's mental conformation has changed for the worse is based on nothing more substantial than that which would best be described as a vibe. I respect my vibes. When I'm in good form, my vibes are impeccable. When I'm not, they suck. However, I've learned the hard way that they are not to be ignored. Most of the time I don't bet because of a bad vibe, I end up on the right side of the ledger. The best way to think of a vibe is that we all have a thin, porous membrane that separates our consciousness from reality. All the inchoate, unprocessed information that seeps through that membrane and never crystallizes, if indeed it ever does, into a knowable concept, makes its presence known as a vibe.

****

A horse's class can also be subject to change. Every so often, I see a horse in good form getting 'put away' by horses he previously would have dominated with ease. As to why this is? It's just another question for which I have no answer.

I recall a multiple Grade I Stakes winner, a turf horse who won at classic distances at both Belmont and Gulfstream, the sort who was most steadfast and loath to give an inch in the drive to the wire, finishing his career getting put away by $1,500 claimers at a third-rate venue. He was a gelding and had no value at stud, so they kept racing him. It was a sad ending. It brought to mind Joe Louis performing in the wrestling ring, trying to make ends meet when his boxing skills had eroded to the point that he could no longer be competitive against those he would have previously toyed with when he was in just so-so form.

On occasion, a horse that has never shown much class commences stamping his will upon those that formerly would have easily taken his measure. As to why this happens, again, I have no idea. I simply go with the flow and react accordingly. Like I said, things change.

A horse likes a distance or a racing surface, chances are he will always like them. His form in this regard simply doesn't change. When a horse loses at a distance or on a surface that he has shown in the past he likes, I know it is not the distance or the surface that has caused the poor showing.

****

A professional sort gets my full attention when his connections wheel him right back and enter him a day or two after he has put in a 'monster' effort. Obviously, his connections feel that their charge's recent effort has taken little out of him and that he is sitting on dead ready. I respect the trainer and know this sort of move is part of his repertoire, I'll bet.

Once, I was sick. Had a slight fever. A horse I had a positive, productive history with was being wheeled back three days after a loss where he had a legitimate excuse. He had been full of run but got blocked along the rail, then upon extricating himself from that predicament, clipped heels, whereupon his jockey simply eased off him, and he finished up the track, badly beaten. It was before OTB. If I wanted to bet, I had to get up out of a sick bed and drive to Aqueduct. Though Spring, it was a cold, windy, raw, sunless day. The wind chill was in the low twenties. My wife was beside herself. She couldn't believe I was going. I went. I won. When I got home, I was in bad shape. I was weak as a baby and had a high fever. We had to call the Doctor. Those days, doctors made house visits. He gave me so many shots that I felt like a pin cushion. Turned out I had pneumonia. My wife told the Doctor about my going to the track. He just shook his head as if he pitied me.

"But the horse won," I said, believing that exonerated me from further castigation. He paid "seventeen and change."

The Doctor, now in lecturing mode, told me that not only was I a danger to myself, but I was also a danger to others, as I could have infected innocent bystanders. I tried to look shamefaced. It was a week before I was able to get out of bed and walk around.

****

'In and out' horses are one of the banes of my racetrack existence. I will not bet on or against an 'in and out' horse with counterfeit money. 'In and out' horses run like professionals one race, then next time out they appear as if they would be hard-pressed to win a race at a county fair in a Maiden race for Clydesdales. 'In and out' horses are random events waiting to happen, wild cards, one of uncertainty's embodiments. I find it impossible to get a grip on their form. They are the quintessential flies in the ointment. Consistency is not part of their vocabulary. One day they are abysmal; the next race they are superb. Awesome one race, a 'dead piece' the next; they play havoc with my plans. Figuring them out is like picking a candy out of a box of chocolates. You never know what you are going to get. When I see them in a race where I like a horse, their presence casts a pall over the proceedings. I've concluded that the only way to figure them out is not to. They are my nemesis. Upsetting my apple cart is their specialty. I'd like to see them declared persona non grata and banned. If I sound a bit paranoid about these horses, it is only because I am. My bank account bears the scars of their perfidy. If I bet on such a horse after they have put in a big effort, they run like turtles. If I bet against them off a woeful effort or two, concluding their form has withered to the point they cannot possibly be a threat, they put in a 'giant' effort and hand me a puzzling, disconcerting defeat. I have come to believe, as silly as it seems, that 'in and out' horses not only enjoy confounding me, but enjoy, even more so, rubbing salt in my wounds.

A horse is said to 'bounce,' it means that after a particularly hard race, his form regresses due to the intensity of the effort he expended. The assumption being that the rigors of the race will have been of such magnitude, taken so much out of him that he will be unable to replicate a similar effort next time he races, much less improve upon it. In terms of his form, he will move backward, not forward. A lot of people believe in the 'bounce.' They respect the notion and give it great credence. Sometimes I hear so much talk of bouncing at the racetrack that I think I'm at a convention of trampoline enthusiasts. I'm not all that into bouncing. Sometimes, after a horse has been hard-used, it might well take something out of him. However, sometimes such an effort might move him forward, be of benefit, improve him, and put something into him that was needed and wasn't there before. As for the bounce's predictive value, I find it wanting. If I had a dollar for every time a horse improved and won off a big effort, I could easily pay off the sovereign debt of a spendthrift third-world country.

Believing in the 'bounce,' I think might well be a reflection of a person's general outlook on life. Bounce people see the glass as half empty. I see it, until proven otherwise, as half full. I see a scintillating performance as a good sign. Bounce enthusiasts see it as ominous.

The only people who have a handle on whether or not an effort has adversely impacted a horse's form are his connections: his trainer, groom, rider, etc. They're the ones with meaningful access to a horse. Is he eating up everything in sight? Or is he off his feed? When he works, does he do what is asked? Is he full of himself? I would love to know the data points that bounce enthusiasts utilize to conclude that a horse will bounce.

Some 'bounce' enthusiasts talk as if the 'bounce' is the ultimate key. Unfortunately for them, by reflexively defaulting to the bounce to explain a poor performance, they mitigate any chance they might have of coming up with the real key. Maybe it was the distance, the surface, the pace, etc.?

When race after race, someone always explains a losing effort to me by declaring that the horse bounced, I commence having the same confidence in his opinion as I would have in the opinion of a doctor who, when making his rounds, offers up the same diagnosis for all of his patients, irrespective of their symptoms.

A horse runs big off a lay-off 'bounce', enthusiasts reflexively avoid the animal the next time he races. Call me old-fashioned if you will, but if a horse on my radar, a professional sort, commences a new campaign with a big effort, especially if it occurs in his prime years, I am sanguine about his future. They aren't. But that's what makes a horse race.

****

In assessing a horse's form, I pay no attention to workouts. If a horse with 'winning ways' is in good form and winning, I assume his works are what his trainer believes is required in order for him to maintain his current good form. Any horse player who thinks he knows the purpose, meaning, and value of a morning workout is, at a minimum, severely ill-advised.

The closest one can come to gathering real-time information as to a horse's form is by perusing his appearance in the paddock and post-parade. The way a horse looks and acts, his deportment, and demeanor just before he competes, can speak volumes as to the state of his competitive juices and the sort of effort he is likely to put forth.

Checking out a horse in the paddock area is not part of my selection process. It is about validating my selection. I go to the paddock, and the horse I like looks woeful, I keep my hands in my pockets.

If I do not think highly of a horse, no matter how awesome he appears, I will not wager on him based solely on the way he is acting in the paddock. I had a dollar for every horse that looked the part in the walking ring and then ran up the track, well, you know, I'd be doing okay. Certainly, no money worries.

I like a horse; I want to see his coat glowing with vigor, shining as if burnished. I want to see him on his toes, prancing, a bit feisty, a touch rambunctious, yet poised, calm, confident, and under control. I want my horse to look like he thinks he's the bee's knees, the cat's meow, and all that. I want to see his head held high, ears pricked. I like a bowed neck. I want him to gaze out at the world through imperious eyes. I want to see his tail held high, proudly defiant, as if it were the regimental flag and he was charged with carrying it into battle.

In the post-parade, I want to see a horse tugging at the bit, like a rambunctious dog straining against the leash. I want him to look tense, coiled, a hair trigger waiting to be pulled, yet again, poised and under control.

What I don't want to see is a horse that looks like a loser. A woebegone chump that looks devoid of fight and appears as if he can think of a thousand places he would rather be. I don't care for a horse that appears listless and disinterested, with his head down as if he has already run up the white flag. I want to see the horse I favor chomping at the bit with zest and glee. I don't want to see him plodding around the walking ring like he is pulling a Hansom cab in Central Park on a stifling hot summer's day. I don't like it if a horse looks doleful.

I would like to say I am able to spot a sore or 'ouchy' horse, but I can't. I'm not a professional horseman, so I can only assume, provided, of course, the stewards don't scratch him, that the horse I like is sound and I am getting a fair shake.

Not all horses look like they came from central casting. Kelso, to put it mildly, looked beyond nondescript. So when I saw Kelso looking nondescript, it didn't bother me one bit, as that was Kelso. On the other hand, if I went to the walking ring and saw, let's say, Slew of Gold, who was one of the handsomest, most impressive-looking thoroughbreds I've ever seen, not looking like his usually awesome self, I would have all sorts of second thoughts as to betting on him.

I cast a jaundiced eye on a horse that is lathered. It might be an indication his nerves have already used him up a touch and he's leaving a bit too much of his race in the walking ring. However, if it is a hot, humid day and all the participants are lathered, I pay it no heed. However, if it is a beautiful Spring Day, with no humidity, with a soft, gentle breeze, a clear blue sky, and the horse I think is the best is the only one lathered, I wash my hands of him and treat him as if he were a leper with smallpox.

Connections

Trainers are craftsmen. They're marching orders; have their minions realize their full potential and be the best racehorses they can be. No such thing as equity or equal outcomes in horse racing. Some trainers are better than others; their handiwork superior. Some trainers routinely turn sow's ears into silk purses. Others do not. They have the opposite effect. They turn silk purses into sow's ears.

The extent to which a horse reaches his potential is a combination of his nature and nurture. A horse's genes supply a horse's nature; his trainer does the nurturing. A trainer ministers to his horse's needs on a daily basis. He keeps him fit, prepares him to compete, and then chooses when and where he will race.

In my experience, horses that win more than their fair share are apt to be associated with trainers who do the same. Though correlation does not necessarily imply causation, usually where there's smoke, there's fire. Consequently, trainers influence my decision-making. If I like a horse and he is managed by a trainer I respect, I am that much more confident that I am doing the right thing when I invest in his chances.

There is a city-operated hospital in Brooklyn, New York, whose name I will not mention. It is said of this hospital that once you go in, no matter for what, a hangnail, a head cold, whatever, there is an excellent chance that you will come out in far worse condition than when you were admitted. Its morbidity rate is off the charts. If I were in a car accident, seriously injured, and that hospital's ambulance was the first on the scene, I'd say, "Thanks, but no thanks." My approach would be to hope and pray that an ambulance from another hospital will appear on the scene before I bled out. Just as it is good to know which hospital will do a patient more harm than good, it is good to know which trainers have the ability to turn a horse who has been hitting on all cylinders into a 'dead piece.' I become leery when a legitimate sort of horse, enjoying excellent, winning form, finds his way into the barn of a trainer I consider an abject loser.

A horse changes barns, finds himself in the hands of a trainer that I do not hold in high esteem, and then wins at first asking for his new connection; I'm still not convinced. Lots of times, a horse wins for his new connections, it is because of what his previous trainer did. A horse goes from a winning barn to one that is anything but, I find myself waiting for the other shoe to drop.

As to why certain trainers have less success than others, I have no idea. All I know is that if I glance at the standings and see that at the current meet a trainer has entered 38 horses and won only twice, what more do I have to know as per my chances of collecting on a horse he is overseeing?

A tip-off that a trainer is a loser, besides, of course, the fact that he rarely wins, is that when he takes control of a professional sort, the horse not only loses his physical form but his intangibles suffer as well, and he seems to cease caring one way or the other if he dominates and wins. When a horse's mental conformation undergoes such a transformation upon changing barns, it is not as if those intangibles are then lost forever. Sometimes it is as if they lay dormant, as if hibernating, awaiting the hand of another trainer, one with a different approach. Such horses, for whatever reason, find their way into the barn of a trainer who I have seen in the past rehabilitate such horses, I pay careful attention as his ministrations might be the antidote that will reawaken the horse's desire to win and bring them back to life, same as what happened to Sleeping Beauty when she awoke from her slumber upon being kissed by Prince Charming.

A horse with 'winning ways' finds his way into a barn that wins less than its fair share and he still continues to win; I give the horse all sorts of respect. Why? Having to overcome a trainer who isn't the sharpest tool in the shed is a lot of adversity for a horse to overcome, a true hurdle.

A tip-off that a trainer has a clue is that if upon assuming management of a horse that has been an inveterate loser and a non-factor throughout his entire career, the horse evolves into a force to be reckoned with and turns into a real racehorse. A trainer puts me in a position where I find myself assiduously following a horse in his care that I had long considered to be a no account, a ne'er do well. I take note. Certain trainers have a green thumb when it comes to getting horses to bloom. I know who they are. You figure it out. This does not automatically mean that a top-notch trainer will always get the best out of a horse. No one is perfect. Some horses, sadly, are irredeemable.

A horse leaves a barn where he has been woeful, a non-factor, and finds himself back in a barn where he once comported himself as a professional, I pay attention. Oftentimes, it is just what the Doctor ordered.

A woeful sort goes from a trainer that wins less than his fair share to another trainer with a similar resume, I pay him no attention. What for?

Good trainers seem to age like fine wine, and most of the good ones have been around awhile. Training thoroughbreds is very competitive. The big money in play makes for a highly disciplined marketplace. Just because someone sets up shop and says he's a trainer doesn't necessarily make him one. He has to prove it. He has to get clients to entrust him with their stock and then add value to their investment. Trainers that can't get the job done are soon culled, same as horses that don't have a clue.

The quality of the stock a trainer has in his barn is a critical variable. The better the stock, the better the horse's genes, the better a trainer's chances of winning. That being said, there is a reason why some trainers get to work with superior stock and others do not. It is part of the discipline the market imposes. If I were an owner and I invested heavily in horseflesh with an eye toward maximizing and enhancing my investment, I would seek out a trainer who had demonstrated his ability to do so. Horses are not only expensive assets; they are also costly to maintain. It's not like owning a cat. I got my cat for nothing at an animal shelter. Purchasing litter and cat food are my only fixed costs. And I don't care if my cat never earns a penny as long as she sleeps on my chest when I take my afternoon nap. I love my cat, and she loves me. She's a closely coupled calico with a kind eye. If I invested a couple of million in horseflesh and hundreds of thousands of dollars maintaining them, I would have an entirely different set of expectations.

Pay careful attention to those trainers that win more than their share, and patterns will emerge. In this guise, I'm like a football coach trying to ascertain another team's tendencies. Being conversant with a trainer's patterns and when and where he is seriously trying to win can be of immense benefit. What better information than knowing a trainer is looking to win at a price? It's almost like a stock trader having insider information. Usually, when I bet, it's about the horse. Sometimes, though, it is more about the trainer and his patterns.

I offer two examples. When Suffolk Downs in Boston was an active venue, known to one and all as 'Sufferin Downs,' the racing stock that competed there was distinctly inferior to the stock stabled on the New York circuit. New Yorkers have a provincial mindset to begin with, and as a general rule, look down on horses shipping in from out of town. They especially looked down on horses shipping in from Suffolk Downs with unbridled contempt and disdain. Suffolk Downs shippers were sneered at and dismissed out of hand. Nine times out of 10, when a horse shipped in from Suffolk Downs to race in New York, he had little impact, confirming and validating the local's opinion as to the worth of Suffolk invaders. Suffolk Downs shippers were always dramatic overlays, and for the most part, rightfully so. People tossed them out with alacrity. However, it came to my attention over the years that there was one Suffolk Downs trainer when he took the time and expense to ship a horse to run in New York, it was in one's best interests to pay careful attention. His horses always ran big. Bet on one of his horses, and you always got a run for your money. Over the long haul, if you bet on that Suffolk-based trainer every time he shipped into New York, you would have been way ahead. Sometimes, because of the New York player's overarching parochialism, his horses paid 'boxcars.'

I'd also kept an especially watchful eye on him when he showed up at Saratoga. I don't think many would argue against the notion that Saratoga is the premier racing meet in North America, if not the world. It attracts the best horses in training. If one wishes to make a statement as to the quality of a horse, one races him or her at Saratoga. Day after day, quality fields are showcased. Invariably, once or twice during the course of the Saratoga meet, the aforementioned Suffolk Downs trainer would ship a horse in. To some that the trainer of a horse stabled at Suffolk Downs had the temerity to ship a horse from that venue to race over Saratoga's hallowed grounds bordered on the blasphemous. The fans would reflexively throw out the Suffolk horse and poke fun at his chances the same way they had laughed at the tortoise the day he toed the starting line against the hare. And they laughed all the harder because the Suffolk horse often appeared to be entered in an improbable spot. Like a $10,000 claimer, a professional sort, but nonetheless, still a $10,000 Suffolk Downs claimer, was spotted against hard knocking sorts that routinely won for $25,000 tags at venues like Belmont, Santa Anita, Churchill Downs, etc.

After the race, they weren't laughing anymore. They were scratching their heads. Not me. I was whistling with glee as I walked to cash my tickets, feeling as I imagine I would if I held up a bank in broad daylight and got away free as a bird with a suitcase full of cash.

I'm not saying this trainer won every time he shipped into Saratoga. But he didn't have to. A trainer races three horses at Saratoga; two of them lose, and the one that wins pays 35–1, one does not have to have gone to MIT and earned a Ph.D. in Applied Mathematics to know that if you had bet on all three, you would have done quite well. As to what his secret sauce was, I had no idea. Nor did I care. All I knew is that when he shipped a runner up to Saratoga, he wasn't tilting at windmills. The wisdom I had assembled over the years as to the method and theory of horse playing became irrelevant. With him, it was all about the trainer, not the horse. He was the key. Betting on such horses had to be approved by the Executive Racing Committee (ERC). I spoke both ardently and eloquently in support of the motion. The Executive Racing Committee (ERC), unanimously agreed with my arguments and gave its stamp of approval.

Another trainer I kept tabs on managed a small yet elite stable of well-bred stock. Invariably, once or twice a year, he would take a horse whose breeding said classic distance on the turf and prep the horse in dirt sprints. In the six-furlong dirt sprints, the colt or filly would flash all sorts of early speed, then go backward. Then one day I'd open the form and see that the colt or filly whose breeding suggested he might well be able to stay a classic distance but who had gotten hammered at six furlongs on the dirt was entered at either a mile and a quarter or a mile or a half on the turf. People would look at the colt's sprints, where he had shown early foot, and then gone backward and dismiss their chances out of hand. Their reasoning being that if the colt or filly couldn't stay six furlongs, how could he possibly get a mile and a quarter, much less a mile and a half? What they didn't integrate into their analysis was that the mile and a quarter on the turf was the objective all along, and winning in those sprints would have been nice, but it wasn't the reason they were entered. It was always a pleasure to behold the fan's bewilderment when the colt went wire to wire and won eased up under wraps.

I know it violates my precept to bet on a horse to do something he has never done before, as well as to bet on lightly raced horses I know little about. But every rule does have its exceptions. And one of my exceptions was that when this trainer did what he did, my rules went out the window. The Executive Racing Committee (ERC) met and gave me an exemption, same as they had with Stage Door Johnny's offspring on the turf. The trainer didn't win every time he utilized this pattern, but I knew what he was up to, and I knew he was nobody's fool. But again, if a trainer loses two out of three and the one winner pays $94.00 to win, I'll take that every day of the week. Again, it wasn't about the colt or filly; it was all about the trainer. Year after year, I had seen him use that pattern to get to the winner's circle. It wasn't like I was expecting him to do something he hadn't already done. Once, I drove down to Monmouth just to make a bet on a colt he'd entered. The colt went off 40–1. I forget the colt's name, but the $82.40 will be etched in my brain for eternity. The car ride home was most pleasant despite the fact that traffic was bumper to bumper the whole way as there was a multiple-car pileup on the Garden State Parkway.

I know one or two trainers who like nothing better than to take a sprinter previously incapable of rating and then getting him to do so. I know of trainers that win a high percentage of races when they ask horses to go from a sprint to a route; trainers that invariably improve a horse off a claim; trainers that are to be reckoned with when they ship a horse in from out of town. There are all sorts of trainers with all sorts of different patterns. I could give you their names, but that would rob you of that sublime, eureka-like moment when you arrive at that conclusion on your own, and the feelings of joy that then ripple through your brain are similar to what would be engendered by a pleasant, yet mild, narcotic.

Some people are into equipment changes. They watch them like a hawk. They get excited when a trainer makes an equipment change. For some, equipment changes seem to have an almost orgasmic effect. When a trainer puts on or takes off the blinkers, puts on or takes off a shadow roll, puts on back bandages, takes them off, puts on front bandages, takes them off, etc., they see it as a key, a hinge point.

When I worked as a hot walker and I saw my trainer or any of the trainers we shared our barn with changing equipment, it was usually because they were flailing and were at the point where they would try anything to get the horse in question to change his attitude and behave like a real racehorse. Also, I learned that nine times out of ten, a trainer fiddles with a loser's equipment, it makes no difference. The horse still loses. Turning a lemon into lemonade is rarely that easy. I strike up a conversation with someone obsessed with equipment changes, I slowly dissolve into the background.

****

I never let a jockey influence my decision. If I like a horse, I like him no matter his rider. My reasoning is as follows: if I think a horse best and respect his or her trainer, I can only assume that the trainer, a competent, professional horseman, knows precisely what he is doing when selecting the jockey. The trainer has a lot more skin in the game than I do. The decisions he makes, including the selection of a rider, determines his livelihood; whether or not his family has a roof over their heads, food on the table, good stuff like that. If a professional trainer who has demonstrated his competence over the years and has far more riding on the outcome of a race feels a particular jockey suits his charge, who am I to second-guess him? He's a professional horseman, not me. I hear a bettor in the stands decry a trainer's choice of jockey; my mind is boggled by his pretension, presumption, and, well, there is no other way of saying it, ignorance.

A gregarious sort, always willing to listen and learn, I have been known to strike up conversations at the races and chat with utter strangers. When all an individual can talk about is jockeys and his decision-making process is based on who is riding whom, I find an excuse to go elsewhere, as I know I am in the presence of a brain that is not worth picking.

The sad part is that folks who can't see past the jockeys are obviously not seeing the races for what they are. They're missing out. The potential for their intellectual growth in this area, along with the concomitant development of their insight and understanding, is hamstrung. It's like going to the Louvre, glancing at the paintings, and focusing on the frames. One might get a better understanding of frames, but it's the paintings that have something special to say.

The only exception to my attitude toward jockeys involves magic. Allow me to explain. I play golf. Every so often, I find that I'm in a zone. My drives all find the middle of the fairway. My irons are towering darts that hit green after green as if laser-guided. I get up and down out of the sand with ease. I drain every putt. My confidence knows no bounds. I'm in control. It's all me. I feel it. As to why this happens, I have no idea. The only way I can explain it, I'm magical. I'm in a zone from which I know not how or why I arrived. Unfortunately, magic comes and goes, sort of like luck, and it can leave you quickly without warning.

Occasionally, I get magical at the racetrack. Whatever move I make is the right move. Every decision is spot on. I can do no wrong. Race after race, I see the future. It's wonderful. Once, I went almost two weeks without a losing day. Why? I don't know. Perhaps the stars were in a unique alignment. And then, just like that, I couldn't cash a ticket if my life depended on it.

Every so often, a trainer gets hot, magical, whatever you want to call it, and whatever horse he sends out wins. If a barn gets magical, I like one of their horses, I like them that much more.

Jockeys as well can get magical. A jockey gets magical; it builds on itself, the same as a feedback loop. Trainers know which jockey is magical and which is not. If a trainer has a horse sitting on dead ready, and wants to grab a purse, he will, if he can, engage the hot, magical jockey. I like a horse; his jockey is magical. I like him all that much more.

The most magical I ever saw a jockey was Stevie Cauthen in the late '70s. For several months, he would routinely, in a matter-of-fact fashion, as if it were no big deal, win five or six races every day. It was almost like a given. And then one day he decided he wanted to ply his trade elsewhere, and he packed up his tack and went to California. I guess his magic couldn't get a boarding pass because not a scintilla of it followed. It was soon apparent he couldn't win a race no matter what. It got so bad that Laz Barrera took him off Affirmed. From being the most magical jockey ever, in a few short weeks he became devoid of any and all magic. It was sad, strange, and befuddling.

****

A word about the 'hot money.' 'Hot money' is the money that is bet late.

Some people get all worked up over the 'hot money.' They see it as 'smart money,' money that is in the know. They assume a barn is looking to make a score. For example, eight minutes to post a horse drops from 8–1 to 5–1. Then two minutes later, he drops to 7–2. The fans, lemmings that some of them are, stampede to the windows. The horse goes off 7–5 and loses.

All I'll say about 'the hot money, the smart money', is that if every time the 'hot money' lost, I was awarded a mere dollar, I would be richer than Rockefeller. I have no respect for people who follow the 'hot money.' They're sheep. And sheep get sheared.

When I was a hot walker, one day I was walking one of our fillies around the walking ring. Suddenly, she got all the hot money. In the space of 10 minutes, she went from 15–1 to 8–5. I was puzzled. The trainer was perplexed. The owner kept asking the trainer if the trainer knew something that he should know as it was his filly. The filly ran up the track at 1–2. She was a sweet horse, my favorite. I actually think she liked me and enjoyed my company. With me, she was like a big, friendly, 950 lb. dog. But we certainly didn't expect her to win that day. As far as we were concerned the race was a prep. How or why she got all the 'hot money' and went off odds-on that day is something that is beyond me. But I think it tells you all you need to know about the 'hot money.' For several days after her getting all the late money, it was the main topic of conversation around the barn. We never figured it out. And we, the barn, were theoretically the source that knew she was sitting on dead-ready and she was going to run a big race.

The only way I can explain the 'hot money' is the way some have theorized how a Hurricane might come into being. One tiny event, like a butterfly fluttering his wings off the coast of West Africa, sets off a ripple effect that cascades through the atmosphere, and two months later a monster of a hurricane barrels into the Gulf Coast. The same sort of thing might well set off the 'hot money.' Like someone bumps their head on something, gets a touch dizzy, and while his mind is a bit clouded, he believes he hears someone whisper to a friend that such and such a barn is going to tap out on such and such a horse in the seventh at Belmont, and then he tells a friend, who tells another friend or two, and so on and so forth.

Speed Handicapping
Fool's Gold

There are differing schools of thought as to how one can best perceive and understand a horse race. Of late, one school of thought has taken hold and embedded its orthodoxies, much like a cult, in a significant portion of the fan base. Its practitioners refer to themselves as speed handicappers. The reason, I believe, for the popularity of their approach lies in the fact that it doesn't require a whole lot of thought to become one of its savants. All one needs to know in order to grasp horse racing's mysteries is the ability to add and subtract.

In this final chapter, I explore and critique the foundations upon which speed handicapping is built.

Speed handicapping is very much in vogue. Due to the clamoring of speed handicapping enthusiasts, many tracks now list a race's final times in hundredths of a second rather than the fifth of a second that used to be the norm. Some speed handicapper's 'numbers' are considered to be of such value that people pay good money to access them. This brings to mind what H.L. Mencken noted when he said, "No one has ever lost money underestimating the intelligence of the American public."

In the first paragraph of this book, I reference the Sapir-Whorf Hypothesis, which posits the notion that language structures reality and that words are the prism through which we access and organize the world.

With this as context, I'm of the strong opinion that seeing and understanding a horse race through a prism of numbers detracts rather than adds to one's understanding and appreciation of the sport. Viewing a horse race in terms of numbers distorts and damages its aesthetics and meaning, the same as a fun house mirror plays havoc with its' reflections. Horses are horses, numbers are numbers. When you attempt to transform the former into the latter, much of its meaning is lost in translation, eviscerated, obscured, and the potential emotional and intellectual enrichment that is there for the asking is reduced to a farthing. It is a reductionist approach and a rather crass one at that. By engaging in such a tactic, reducing a horse to a 'number,' it keeps that which is meaningful at arm's length and obscures rather than enhances one's understanding of the sport. It's fool's gold.

I'm not knocking numbers. In certain contexts, reducing reality to numbers has illuminated and advanced our understandings, as certain segments of reality lend themselves to exegesis via numbers: mathematics, chemistry, physics, profits and losses, etc. If it weren't for numbers, we wouldn't be able to put men on the moon, enjoy conversations with friends in New York via cellphone while dining in Florence, access our genome, surf the internet, or grasp the nature of quantum mechanics.

What speed handicappers don't seem to grasp is that certain orders of phenomena lend themselves to mathematical analysis, while others do not. Horse racing does not.

Using numbers to apprehend and elucidate a collective work of art, which horse racing most certainly is, impairs rather than clarifies one's vision. When I gaze at the Brooklyn Bridge, I don't see numbers; I see a stunningly elegant reflection of our collective imagination.

The reason speed handicappers reach out to numbers for salvation like drowning men seeking a lifeline is because they simply do not understand what horse racing is all about, its meanings, and that which it seeks to tell us about certain elementary aspects of the human condition. Numbers do not make my spirit soar and leave me enthralled. Horse racing does, and that's what it is all about.

In my opinion, the key foundational mistake on which speed handicapping is built is the belief that horses race to find out who's fastest. Therefore, they believe the best way to measure a horse is in terms of how fast he is able to run, as manifested by the times that he posts. I'm of the steadfast belief that horses do not race to see who is fastest, but rather who is best. Being the fastest and being the best are not one in the same. Granted, being fleet afoot certainly helps a horse to demonstrate that he is indeed the best, but it is not the end all and be all.

Speed handicappers are of the belief that the principle impediment to their conjuring up an endless conveyor belt of winners is the problem posed by attempting to compare the times generated on different days at different tracks. As noted earlier, track surfaces can vary from one day to the next in their ability to tire a horse, which in turn impacts the times that are produced. The issue for speed handicappers, both their Holy Grail and Rosetta Stone, is how does one go about comparing a time run at Belmont when the going was glib and fast times were the norm, with times generated at, let's say, Laurel, on a day when the track was tiring and slow times were the order of the day.

In response to this problem, to ameliorate it, to allow disparate times to be compared, and in so doing, to reveal who's fastest, speed handicappers have come up with a mathematical construct called a Speed Variant. Speed Variants supposedly allow its adherents to meaningfully compare times produced on different days at different tracks, and, in so doing, elucidate who is fastest, not best, which are two completely different things.

I'm not going to discuss or critique the methodology that speed handicappers use to arrive at their track variants. Suffice to say that I find their methods and reasoning sophisticated and, at times, bordering on elegant. Their logic is impeccable and internally consistent. In fact, I believe, as much as it is possible, that they have indeed solved the problem of comparing times.

The problem with their approach resides in the foundations on which it is built: that horses race to see who is fastest. From this flawed axiomatic notion flows the belief that numbers, which supposedly measure how fast a horse ran, offer the most meaningful and compelling metric to discern a horse's worth. As their basic premise, that horses race to see who is fastest, is seriously flawed, all subsequent principles deduced from that notion are tainted as well.

I believe I've successfully argued in previous chapters that there are any number of factors, none of them having anything to do with how fast a horse is capable of running, that can determine a race's outcome: a horse's class, the intensity of his or her 'winning ways,' the pace, the surface, the distance, the 'trip' incurred, current form, etc.

A horse's time isn't created in a vacuum. All numbers tell you is how much time elapsed for a horse to get from Point A, the starting gate, to Point B, the finish line. All such numbers tell me is, well, a horse's numbers. What I wish to grasp are the race's dynamics, the underlying functions that created and determined the outcome and revealed who was best that day, the winner.

To flesh out the point I'm trying to make as to how fast a horse can run are irrelevant, I again address 'morning glories,' as they speak most eloquently as to the issue of whether or not there is a correlation between a horse's ability to run fast and his being the best. 'Morning glories' run holes in the wind in their morning workouts. They register one bullet work after another. When running against the clock, they show all sorts of brilliance. Their moves can astound. I've seen 'morning glories' put in works that toyed with track records. But then, come the afternoon, they finish up the track, badly beaten.

I pose the following question: if being able to run fast is that meaningful a metric for measuring a horse's worth, why is it that 'morning glories,' who can run quite fast, as evidenced by their works, do not win races?

Speed handicappers, when defending their opinion, are fond of saying, "Numbers don't lie." This is true; numbers don't lie. But if you're measuring that which has little to no meaning, it's worse than a lie; it's moot and pointless.

If the numbers folks could come up with 'numbers' that could accurately assess a horse's class, his will to win, they would have my full attention and then some. Why? Because they're critical components in determining who's best. Not fastest, best. Had speed handicappers commenced their quest to impose mathematical rigor to horse racing with the assumption that horses race to see whose best, not fastest, perhaps then they might have come up with something that has meaning and adds value.

I will concede that if indeed horses ran as fast as they could every time they raced, perhaps then 'numbers' as mediated by Track Variants might provide a meaningful metric. But that is simply not the case. Race after race, factors come into play which preclude a horse from running as fast as he can. If the speed handicappers had additional numbers, they could embed in their formulas to ameliorate and account for the other exigencies that intrude on a horse's performance; perhaps then their numbers might mean something. But such is not the case.

With this as context, I would like to explore several scenarios where horses do not run as fast as they can.

First query: What do 'numbers' tell me about the worth and potential of legitimate professionals, winners, who run only as fast as they have to? In such a case, the number a horse posts is not so much a function of how fast he is capable of running, but rather how fast he had to run in order to win. Two very different things. When a horse is eased up under wraps from the 1/8th pole on in after dominating the field, do the speed handicappers have numbers that they can use to adjust their Track Variant so that it reveals just how fast the horse could have run if he wasn't eased up? This leads to asking questions that are unanswerable, like exactly how much was the horse eased up, a little, a lot, a whole lot, and exactly how much is a little, a lot, and a whole lot, etc. in terms of time elapsed. Figure that out, and I will tip my hat to you.

Look at Affirmed. Do you think he ran as fast as he could in every race? No! He'd boss the field, let them know who was in charge, and then he'd go as he pleased to the wire. He was the sort, as many racehorses are, who put a length on the field and then makes it stick.

Rather than finding meaning in such a horse's performance via a number whose meaning is problematic at best, here's what I would take from such a performance where a horse was eased up and didn't have to extend himself to his utmost in order for him to demonstrate his prowess. First off, I'd take note of the horses he beat, and how easily he did so. Certainly, such an analysis, more art than science, would tell me more about the winner's quality than some number plucked out of the air. I would also take note of how the pace impacted his victory. Did it help him or hurt him, and if so, to what degree, all of which would further underscore my understanding as to his current form. If the pace aided and abetted his winning, then I would be a touch less impressed by his victory. If it offered up adversity, which he overcame, then I would be that much more impressed, and my opinion as to his current worth would move up a notch or two. Also, I would have learned for future reference that he liked both the surface and the distance. It seems to me that my approach reveals a heck of a lot more pertinent, interesting, and compelling information, all of which I believe is far more informative than a 'number' of somewhat dubious provenance.

In an earlier chapter, when I discussed the concept of class, I quoted Hall of Fame trainer Preston Burch when he said, "A horse with little class has only to run a few hundred feet alongside a horse that has class, and he'll pull himself up like someone stepping on the brakes." The phenomenon that Burch is referring to is what transpires when a horse gets outclassed and is 'put away.' When a horse is dominated by a classier foe, it's almost as if his competitive juices are short-circuited, and he ceases to compete as ardently as he would have if he had not been dominated. He certainly will not run as fast as he could if he had not been deterred and demoralized by the classier foe he had the misfortune to hook.

If such a situation comes to pass, I find meaning not in the number the dominated horse posted but rather in how the event hints at his overall place in the pecking order.

As for the classy horse, the one who put it the other way, he certainly didn't run as fast as he could for the simple reason he didn't have to.

Is their number out there in the speed handicapper's arsenal that can allow him to adjust their 'number' so it takes into account the impact that a horse dominating a field has on both the horse doing the dominating and those dominated? For example, could they tell me how fast Kelso could have run if the occasion called for it? Or how fast Kelso's competition would have run if they hadn't been outclassed and put away. I think not. When one overlooks the effect that a horse's class has on a horse's performance as well as the competition, one is eliminating from their calculus that which is at the heart and soul of the sport. If racing has a moment of truth, it occurs when horses 'hook up' and throw down, as that is when and where we find out whose best. Not fastest, whose best.

The other day, I'm at the track. I find myself engaged in conversation with a gentleman who swears by his 'numbers.' He purchases them from a professional speed handicapper whose numbers are supposedly distilled from the ultimate, most refined, sophisticated, super-duper track variants. My acquaintance, who has yet to achieve friend status, refers to his 'numbers' as the 'truth.' We discussed the upcoming race. We are both in agreement that it is a two-horse affair. He, naturally, likes the horse with the higher numbers. In the last three races, the horse he likes has put up 'numbers' of 106, 102, and 103, albeit in races where he was the class of the field. I tell him who I like. He checks out the numbers of the horse I favor. In the last three races, the horse I like posted lesser numbers: 96, 94, and 98. He says the horse I like has no chance as his numbers don't compare. He states that the horse he likes is at least three to four lengths better. He smugly notes that 'numbers don't lie.'

I see the race from a somewhat different perspective. No numbers. Both are veteran campaigners. I know them well. Both have winning ways. Both like the surface and the distance and are in good form, and I don't believe the pace will help or hurt either of them to any significant degree. The horse I like is a frontrunner who can rate. He runs only as fast as he has to. He's the sort who likes to put a length on the opposition and make it stick. The other horse is a stalker. However, from what I've seen over the years, the horse I like is one tough customer. Tougher than the other horse and classier. Once on the lead, he does not easily cede it. The other horse is a nice kind of horse, a legitimate sort. I both like and respect him. I've bet on him in the past. In fact, I've won with him. However, from what I've seen of him, he simply does not have the resolve, the heart, the class, and quality to get by the horse I deem best. It's that simple. I think the other horse is better. What can a number tell me that is better than that?

The horse I like, the frontrunner who can rate, shakes off, as anticipated, the feeble efforts of one or two erstwhile front runners. He puts them in their place within the first $1/8^{th}$ of a mile. He's used himself a touch, but nothing that should impact the race's outcome. The stalker takes a trailing position about a length back. At the ½ mile pole, the stalker who sports the higher numbers picks up his pace, quickens, and commences his assault. Midway round the turn, he ranges up alongside the horse I like. The guy who loves the challenger, the horse with higher numbers, looks at me with a knowing, condescending grin and says, "It's over now." My horse, like I said, is a dead game, and as always, he doesn't disappoint. Like the bulldog he is, he digs in for a fight. They engage in earnest, the stalker trying to get by, my horse simply refusing to let him put his head in front. Both are under a hard drive. They ding-dong it. At the $1/8^{th}$ pole, the stalker wilts and retires from the fray, having come to the realization that no matter how hard he tries, the other horse will always have an answer. The horse on the lead, having made his point, his challenger defeated, throttles back, and they go like that to the wire. My horse wins by a length. His numbers didn't foretell his victory; his class did.

I turn to the 'numbers' guy and inform him, "It's over now." Which I consider a very good gloat. As I understand it, good and proper gloating is delivered in soft, dulcet tones. I find loud, egregious gloats a bit boorish and off-putting. Gloats are best delivered with a velvet glove, not an iron fist. I got my gloating skills from Mother. She could gloat with the best of them.

I encountered the same fellow a few days later. I bring up the race. He is so perplexed by the outcome that I actually find myself feeling sorry for the guy, and I decide that even though I am brimming with schadenfreude at his befuddlement to keep my glee to myself.

He just got his 'numbers' for the day the race under discussion took place. Not only did his horse, the one with the far superior 'numbers' lose, but he lost in a time that, when deconstructed via 'the truth,' the track variant, came out as an 87. Yet he lost. The horse he liked had just run three races with numbers over 100. How could that be? He decides the horse must have 'bounced.' He refuses to acknowledge that the key to understanding the result was the relative class of the horses involved, not the 'numbers' they posted. I try to explain the notion of class. He looks at me like I have six heads.

Another issue that speed handicapper's 'numbers' don't address. How do you compare the times a horse posts on a surface he doesn't like with the numbers that he generates, at the same distance, on a racing surface he adores? Is there a number that can be factored into a Track Variant that tells you how much a horse improves or regresses based on the surface? The answer is no.

Also, how do you go about comparing times run at different distances?

Another problem not addressed by speed handicapping's methodology is that the final time a horse posts is very much a function of the pace. This being the case, what possible meaning can a horse's final time have if the pace isn't taken into account? Times aren't produced in a vacuum. For example, what meaning is to be found in the number a frontrunner generates if he gets involved in a speed duel, is hard-used early, and finds himself going in the wrong direction before he even hits the half-mile pole? Do the speed handicappers have a number that they can factor in that reveals how much the speed duel took out of him? What I believe one should glean from such a performance does not reside in the number the horse posted but rather in the fact that he was unable to rate and got chewed up in a speed duel by better horses.

Also, I fail to see how a number can measure the worth of a horse who closes, as his 'numbers' are a function not of how fast he is capable of running but rather the pace he is obliged to run into. A closer runs into a dawdling pace, the number he posts will be somewhat pedestrian. He closes into a fast pace; he'll post a high number. Whatever meaning is to be derived from such an effort is not from the number the closer posted, but the context, the pace in which it was produced. The only insight one can gain from the number a closer is awarded is that it's the 'number' the closer was awarded.

Another issue, of what possible pertinence and meaning can be found in the numbers generated by horses who lack 'winning ways': 'rats,' 'hanging dogs,' and those afflicted with 'seconditis,' etc. Using the numbers of a horse who doesn't have 'winning ways' to determine whether he's going to win makes no sense, not to me.

In the speed handicapper's universe, any aspect of reality can be reduced to a number, and once quantified, equivalencies are immediately rendered between it and other aspects of reality that have also been reduced to a number.

Using this mode of thought, the weight a horse carries, already denoted by a number, is low-hanging fruit and easily integrated into the world view of a speed handicapper, where weight, lengths, and times all become functions that can be expressed numerically. For the speed handicapper, a $1/5^{th}$ of a second, a length, three lbs in a sprint and five lbs in a route are all equal to one. Thus, lengths, times, and weights become fungible.

A horse runs two lengths back of a winner who posts a 90, he is awarded an 88, as two lengths equals $2/5^{th}$ of a second. When I hear people at the track talking about their numbers, multiplying, dividing, adding, and subtracting, it's what I imagine it is like at an accounting convention.

I'm at the track. The winner of a race at a mile and $1/8^{th}$ wins by a length and posts an 88. The horse who comes second finishes one length in arrears, and as one length is equal to $1/5^{th}$ of a second, which is equal to one, his number as per his Track Variant for the race is 87.

The following week, the same two horses meet, again at a mile and $1/8^{th}$. For whatever reason, the conditions for the race mandate a 12 lb. shift in weight in favor of the horse who came second. According to the speed handicappers, 12 lbs. in a route is equal to 4, which in turn is equal to 4/5ths of a second, which is equal to four lengths. Using these numbers and their putative equivalencies, one is forced to conclude, if one is a believer in such nonsense, that the horse who lost by a length last time will, due to the 12 lb. weight shift, run 4/5ths of a second faster and therefore improve by four lengths relative to the other, and therefore, ipso facto, the horse who lost by a length last time out will win by three lengths today. It's right there in black and white. Numbers don't lie.

A fellow I know who believes that his numbers are the be-all and end-all taps out on the horse that came second the previous week. The key, he says, is the 12 lb. weight shift. He says the horse he likes will win by three lengths. He believes it's not even going to be much of a race.

He's right about one thing: it's not going to be much of a race. Both horses are stalkers. They move in tandem, just as they did the previous week. Not only does the same horse win, he wins again, but this time by three lengths, despite the fact that the 'numbers' predicted he would lose by three lengths. Why, he's the better horse. Call me old-finished, but I much prefer to be conversant with which horse is best rather than with his 'numbers.'

****

There are only two instances when I pay attention to weight. If I think the best horse is only a notch or so better than the competition, but he is being asked to give the others weight as if he was four or five notches better, I won't bet.

In the other instance, when a horse is asked to carry in excess of 126 lbs, it gets my attention, and I think twice before I bet, as there is an old saying at the track, "Weight can stop a freight train," which I buy into.

****

However, all that being said, occasionally one is forced to gauge a horse's quality in terms of times rendered and weight carried when the animal in question is so dominant, so transcendent, that it is not possible to judge him in terms of the horses he beats and the style in which he beats them as he is in a different league, heads, and shoulders above them. When a horse is beyond peerless relative to the competition, the only way to get some sort of handle on his quality is by scrutinizing the times he generates and the weight carried. In '68, this was the only way of defining and understanding Dr. Fager and just how special he was.

In his next-to-last race, a Grade I stakes at a mile at Arlington, he was asked to carry 134 lbs. I can count on my fingers the number of times horses have won under such an impost. Not only did he win, he also set the world's record for a mile. He won, eased up, under wraps. The record stood for close to 40 years. The horse that finally broke it carried a paltry 116 lbs.

Dr. Fager's next race, the last of his luminescent career, was the Grade I Vosburgh at seven furlongs. Took my future wife. We were getting serious. Thought it was only fair to let her know what she was in for if we decided to share our lives. In those days, if a horse harbored a desire to be named sprint champion, it was in his best interests to have the Vosburgh on his resume. When a sprint record is broken at a track, it is usually by 1/5th of a second. An occurrence that takes place perhaps once a decade. The track record for seven furlongs at Aqueduct had stood for close to 20 years. Dr. Fager was assigned 139 lbs. No horse in New York, not in my memory at least, had ever won a Grade I Stake carrying more than 136 lbs. Carrying 139 lbs. Dr. Fager not only won, he broke the track record by a full 5/5ths of a second. In other words, under a 139 lbs. impost, Dr. Fager, in one swell swoop, set a record that normally would take a half-century to be whittled down to the degree that it was that day. Check out Dr. Fager's Vosburgh on YouTube. At the 1/16th pole, his rider clucks to him, and he literally runs out of the frame. The camera pans after him. When it finally caught up to him at the finish line, he had put 15 lengths on the field in the last 1/16th of a mile. I've seen moves, and I've seen moves, but this might be the penultimate move, the most compelling ever made. And he was eased up, again under wraps, the same as he was at Arlington. Dr. Fager's seven-furlong record at Aqueduct stood for close to 50 years. When it was broken, the horse that did so carried 112 lbs. Bottom line, in '68 when Dr. Fager was at his best, any horse that ever lived would have challenged him at equal weights, their best race in hand, Dr. Fager would not only have bested them, he most probably would have toyed with them as well. That year, Dr. Fager was Horse of the Year, Best Older Horse, Best Turf Horse, and Best Sprinter. He is the only horse ever to accomplish that feat. In '68, I saw the best racehorse that ever was, Dr. Fager.

The second-best racehorse I ever saw was Seattle Slew.

This is not a knock on Secretariat. Saying that a horse is not as good as Dr. Fager and Seattle Slew is not a knock. I just can't picture Secretariat beating either of the two for the simple reason that you can't beat what you can't catch. Secretariat beat the same horses, Sham, etc., over and over again. He lost to Angle Light in the Wood and to Onion in the Travers. In my wildest dreams, I cannot see Dr. Fager or Seattle Slew losing to either of them.

As for Secretariat's record-shattering performance in the Belmont. He was the house horse, meaning he was owned by one of the old, moneyed families that had been at the center of the sport for generations. Though awesome and great, he was overhyped. The fact that he was the first horse since Citation to win the Triple Crown added to the buzz. The week leading up to his victory in the Belmont, the track was beyond conducive to rendering fast times. That week, practically every Belmont track record on dirt was broken. The track was set up for him to break the track record, and he did. Secretariat was not the best horse ever, same as Ali was not the greatest of heavyweights. Both caught the public's imagination, got hyped, and did what they had to do. Their myths have evolved into, well, mythic proportions and, like all myths, lost touch with what really was. It would be nice if Dr. Fager or Seattle Slew had, as Dr. Johnson did, a Boswell, someone to chronicle their greatness. But they don't. It's on me.